W9-BJE-593

Quotes and Idea Starters
for
Preaching and Teaching

Quotes and Idea Starters
for
Preaching and Teaching

From *Leadership Journal*

Edward K. Rowell, Editor

Baker Books
A Division of Baker Book House Co
Grand Rapids, Michigan 49516

©1996 by Christianity Today, Inc.

Co published by Christianity Today, Inc. and Baker Books
a division of Baker Book House Company
P.O. Box 6287, Grand Rapids, MI 49516-6287
Distributed by Baker Book House Company

Printed in the United States of America

Library of Congress Cataloging-in-Publication Data

Quips, quotes, and idea starters : from Leadership journal / Edward K.
  Rowell, ed.
      p.   cm.
    Includes index.
    ISBN 0-8010-9024-5
    1. Conduct of life—Quotations, maxims, etc.   I. Rowell, Edward K.
  II. Leadership (Carol Stream, Ill.)
  PN6084.C556Q57   1996   082—
  dc20 96-7147

Introduction

The right quote is a pinch of spice for the sermon. It enhances the other ingredients. Its taste, whether pungent or sweet, can linger long after the preacher has closed the Bible and gone home.

For more than fifteen years, LEADERSHIP has been gathering spicy quotes, as contemporary as today's sports page, as lasting as the church fathers. Our aim is to season both your sermons and your soul. A thoughtful phrase will often break the curse of "sermon block," highlighting your own experience and wisdom in a fresh way.

To make this preaching resource even more useful and time saving, we are providing:

1. *The right to copy.* The publisher grants you the right to copy the quotations and file them in the way that best fits your system.

2. *Topical arrangement.* Quotation books indexed by

author don't help unless you already have a quote in mind and know who said it. But with a topical approach, the quotation is easy to find.

3. *Alternate subjects and index.* Each quote is followed by two alternate subjects in parentheses. Since any good quotation has more than one application, you can find the reference you need indexed under at least three topics.

Some anonymous wag said, "Sermons affect different people in different ways: some rise to go greatly strengthened; some awake greatly rested." The judicious use of catchy quotes and famous phrases will, at the very least, make the nappers wonder what they missed.

We're confident that "the use of this book will increase your effectiveness as you communicate the greatest message of all time."

You can quote me on that.

—*Edward K. Rowell*
Assistant Editor, LEADERSHIP
Editor, PREACHING TODAY
Carol Stream, Illinois

Ability

There is something that is much more scarce, something rarer than ability. It is the ability to recognize ability.
—Robert Half
(Discernment, Gifts)

Abortion

When we consider that women are treated as property, it is degrading to women that we should treat our children as property to be disposed of as we wish.
—Elizabeth Cady Stanton
(Women, Children)

Acceptance

The world has a philosophy that says, "What can't be cured must be endured." Christians have a philosophy that says, "What can't be cured can be enjoyed."
—Joni Eareckson Tada
(Endurance, Suffering)

Do not wish to be anything but what you are, and try to be that perfectly. —Francis de Sales
(Contentment, Lifestyle)

In the world to come, I shall not be asked, "Why were you not Moses?" I shall be asked, "Why were you not Zusya?" —Rabbi Zusya
(Contentment, Envy)

Achievement
When you get to the top of the mountain, your first inclination is not to jump for joy, but to look around.
—James Carville
(Evaluation, Success)

Action
If we are going to wait until every possible hindrance has been removed before we do a work for the Lord, we will never attempt to do anything. —T. J. Bach
(Mission, Boldness)

Advantage
To every disadvantage there is a corresponding advantage. —W. Clement Stone
(Disadvantage, Perspective)

Advent
The best way to prepare for the coming of Christ is never to forget the presence of Christ.
—William Barclay
(Christmas, Second Coming)

Adversity

The good things which belong to prosperity are to be wished, but the good things which belong to adversity are to be admired.
—Seneca
(Prosperity, Character)

Kites rise highest against the wind, not with it.
—Winston Churchill
(Achievement, Success)

He knows not his own strength that hath not met adversity. Heaven prepares good men with crosses.
—Ben Johnson
(Strength, Suffering)

Adversity is often the window of opportunity for change. Few people or organizations want to change when there is prosperity and peace. Major changes are often precipitated by necessity.
—Leith Anderson
(Change, Opportunity)

God loves us in good times and bad . . . But he is even more real in our lives when we are having tough times.
—Joe Gibbs
Former head coach of
the Washington Redskins
(Trials, God's Love)

All the wrong people are against it, so it must be right.
—James Carville
Presidential adviser
(Persecution, Opposition)

By the time I'm climbing back up from going down, I'm already thinking about the next play.

—Joe Namath, Hall of Fame quarterback
(Courage, Discipline)

Age

The error of youth is to believe that intelligence is a substitute for experience, while the error of age is to believe that experience is a substitute for intelligence.

—Lyman Bryson
(Intelligence, Experience)

Age is important no less than youth itself, though in another dress. And as the evening twilight fades away, the sky is filled with stars invisible by day.

—Henry Wadsworth Longfellow
(Growth, Maturity)

Ambition

To be ambitious of true honor and of the real glory and perfection of our nature is the very principle and incentive of virtue; but to be ambitious of titles, place, ceremonial respects, and pageantry, is as vain and little as the things are which we court.

—Sir Philip Sidney
(Honor, Virtue)

The kind of successor I may get may depend a great deal on the kind of predecessor I've been and how I've related to my own predecessor. To reject the past and ignore the future . . . is both selfish and foolish.

—Warren W. Wiersbe
(Past, Future)

The slave has but one master, the ambitious man has as many as there are persons whose aid may contribute to the advancement of his fortunes.　—Jean de la Bruyere
(Freedom, Slavery)

We all want to be great, but we don't want folks to know we want to be great.　—Phil Lineberger
(Pride, Deception)

Keep away from people who try to belittle your ambitions. Small people always do that, but the really great make you feel that you, too, can become great.
—Mark Twain
(Greatness, Criticism)

Anger
Speak when you're angry—and you'll make the best speech you'll ever regret.　—Laurence J. Peter
(Self-control, Tongue)

Anxiety
Anxiety is the great modern plague. But faith can cure it.　—Smiley Blanton
(Faith, Peace)

Apathy

Think about people who find themselves in religious ruts. They discover a number of things about themselves. They will find that they are getting older but not getting any holier. Time is their enemy, not their friend. . . . They were not any better last year than they had been the year before.
—A. W. Tozer
(Holiness, Routine)

Assumptions

Unspoken premises direct the course of any civilization. The ideas which are not even argued are the building blocks of society.
—James Newby
(Civilization, Ideas)

Attitude

It is not so important to be serious as it is to be serious about the important things. The monkey wears an expression of seriousness which would do credit to any scholar, but the monkey is serious because he itches.
—Robert M. Hutchins
(Perspective, Importance)

There are no menial jobs, only menial attitudes.
—William J. Bennett
(Work, Values)

Baptism

In baptism we are initiated, crowned, chosen, embraced, washed, adopted, gifted, reborn, killed, and thereby sent forth and redeemed. We are identified as one of God's own, then assigned our place and our job within the kingdom of God. —William Willimon
(Redemption, Kingdom of God)

Belief

Borrowed beliefs have no power.

—James Black
(Convictions, Power)

Bible

I am a Christian because God says so, and I did what he told me to do, and I stand on God's Word, and if the Book goes down, I'll go with it. —Billy Sunday
(Word of God, Obedience)

It is better to pray over the Bible than to brood over the
self.
—P. T. Forsyth
(Prayer, Self)

The Bible was not given to increase our knowledge but
to change our lives.
—D. L. Moody
(Change, Knowledge)

The Bible is alive, it speaks to me; it has feet, it runs
after me; it has hands, it lays hold of me.
—Martin Luther
(Conviction, Inspiration)

The Bible is a stream of running water, where alike the
elephant may swim, and the lamb walk without losing
its feet.
—Gregory the Great
(Knowledge, Simplicity)

Bitterness
Like the bee, we distill poison from honey for our self-
defense—what happens to the bee if it uses its sting is
well known.
—Dag Hammarskjold
(Gossip, Slander)

Blessing
God is more anxious to bestow his blessings on us than
we are to receive them.
—Augustine
(Gifts, God)

Body of Christ

Alone I cannot serve the Lord effectively, and he will spare no pains to teach me this. He will bring things to an end, allowing doors to close and leaving me ineffectively knocking my head against a wall until I realize that I need the help of the body as well as of the Lord.
—Watchman Nee
(Church, Self-reliance)

There are times when together we discover that we make up a single body, that we belong to each other and that God has called us to be together as a source of life for each other.
—Jean Vanier
(Community, Unity)

Brevity of Life

For weeks after my last operation [for cancer]—frail and without energy, sleeping ten hours—I looked in my house at all the books I had not read and wept for my inability to read them. Or I looked at great books I had read too quickly in my avidity—telling myself I would return to them later. There is never a *later,* but for most of my life I have believed in *later.*
—Donald Hall
(Time, Decisions)

We are always complaining that our days are few and acting as though there would be no end of them.
—Seneca
(Death, Self-deception)

Busyness

If you have so much business to attend to that you have no time to pray, depend upon it, you have more business on hand than God ever intended you should have.

—D. L. Moody
(Prayer, Disobedience)

Lord, I shall be very busy this day. I may forget Thee, but do not Thou forget me.

—Sir Jacob Astley
(Devotion, Forgetfulness)

Calling

O ye gifted ones, follow your calling, let neither obsta-
cles nor temptations induce you to leave it; bound along
if you can; if not, on hands and knees follow it. Turn
into other paths, and, for a momentary advantage or
gratification, ye have sold your inheritance, your immortality.   —George Borrow
                                            (Gifts, Perseverance)

Calm

Christ's life outwardly was one of the most troubled
lives that was ever lived: tempest and tumult, tumult
and tempest, the waves breaking over it all the time. But
the inner life was a sea of glass. The great calm was
always there.   —Henry Drummond
                                                (Trouble, Christ)

Sometimes God calms the storm—and sometimes he lets the storm rage and calms his child.　　　　—Unknown
(Peace, Assurance)

Causes
When great causes are on the move in the world . . . we learn that we are spirits, not animals.
—Winston Churchill
(Beliefs, Human Nature)

Chance
God does not play dice with the universe.
—Albert Einstein
(God, Evolution)

Change
People wish to be settled; only as far as they are unsettled is there any hope for them.　　—Ralph Waldo Emerson
(Hope, Desire)

We trained hard . . . but every time we were beginning to form into teams we would be reorganized. I was to learn later in life that we tend to meet any new situation by reorganizing. And what a wonderful method it can be for creating the illusion of progress while producing inefficiency and demoralization.　　　　—Petronius
(Progress, Organization)

Character
What really matters is what happens in us, not to us.
—James W. Kennedy
(Growth, Difficulty)

Ability will get you to the top, but it takes character to
keep you there. —John Wooden
(Ability, Talent)

The ultimate measure of a man is not where he stands
in moments of comfort and convenience, but where he
stands at times of challenge and controversy.
—Martin Luther King, Jr.
(Adversity, Controversy)

So many missionaries, intent on doing something, forget
that God's main work is to make something of them.
—Jim Elliot
(Missions, Work)

No man can for any considerable time wear one face to
himself and another to the multitude without finally getting bewildered as to which is the true one.
—Nathaniel Hawthorne
(Deception, Honesty)

The proof of Christianity is not a book but a life. The
power of Christianity is not a creed but a Christian
character; and wherever you see life that has been
transformed by the grace of God, you see a witness to
the resurrection of Jesus. —William M. Woodfin
(Witness, Christianity)

It is easy in the world to live after the world's opinion. It
is easy in solitude to live after one's own. But the great
man is he who, in the midst of the crowd, keeps with
perfect sweetness the independence of his character.
—Ralph Waldo Emerson
(Peer Pressure, Independence)

People are like stained-glass windows. They sparkle and shine when the sun is out. But in the darkness, beauty is seen only if there is a light within.　　—Anonymous
(Perseverance, Beauty)

Character is what you are in the dark.
—D. L. Moody
(Consistency, Perseverance)

Blessed is he who has learned to admire but not to envy, to follow but not imitate, to praise but not flatter, and to lead but not manipulate.　　—William Arthur Ward
(Virtue, Blessing)

Do not pray for easy lives; pray to be stronger people! Do not pray for tasks equal to your powers; pray for powers equal to your tasks. Then the doing of your work shall be no miracle, but you shall be a miracle. Every day you shall wonder at yourself, at the richness of life which has come to you by the grace of God.
—Phillips Brooks
(Strength, Perseverance)

When the rock is hard, we get harder than the rock. When the job is tough, we get tougher than the job.
—George Cullum, Sr.
(Perseverance, Toughness)

I would rather be cheated a hundred times than develop a heart of stone.　　—Tim Stafford
(Forgiveness, Heart)

Cheerfulness

It is not fitting, when one is in God's service, to have a gloomy face or a chilling look. —Francis of Assisi
(Gloom, Depression)

Childlikeness

Now, as always, God [discloses] himself to "babes" and hides himself in thick darkness from the wise and the prudent. We must simplify our approach to him. We must strip down to essentials (and they will be found to be blessedly few). We must put away all effort to impress, and come with the guileless candor of childhood. If we do this, without doubt God will quickly respond. —A. W. Tozer
(Prayer, Devotion)

Children

People who do not like children are swine, dunces, and blockheads, not worthy to be called men and women, because they despise the blessing of God, the Creator and Author of marriage. —Martin Luther
(Marriage, Blessing)

Choices

Perpetual devotion to what man calls his business is only to be sustained by perpetual neglect of many other things. —Robert Louis Stevenson
(Devotion, Neglect)

We are ever being born, or dying, and the thrill of choosing which is ours. Only once must we be born without our own consent. Only once must we die without our own permission.
—Calvin Miller
(Birth, Death)

Christ

We read not that Christ ever exercised force but once, and that was to drive profane ones out of his temple, and not to force them in.
—John Milton
(Force, Restraint)

Two things there are which man has no arithmetic to reckon, and no lie to measure. One of these things is the extent of that man's loss who loses his own soul. The other is the extent of God's gift when he gave Christ to sinners . . . Sin must indeed be exceeding sinful, when the Father must needs give his only Son to be the sinner's Friend!
—J. C. Ryle
(Sin, Cross)

The supreme education of the soul comes though an intimate acquaintance with Jesus Christ of history.
—Rufus M. Jones
(Education, Soul)

As every Scot knows, salt must be put into the oatmeal from the start, before cooking, not afterward. In a similar way, Christ can never be added as an afterthought to an already full and committed life. It's possible to attempt to use the Master and his power to fulfill our desires and plans for the people we love and still give him the one position he will not accept: second place.
—Lloyd John Ogilvie
(Character, Commitment)

Christianity

The Christian ideal has not been tried and found wanting. It has been found difficult and left untried.
—G. K. Chesterton
(Idealism, Difficulty)

Christianity is a demanding and serious religion. When it is delivered as easy and amusing, it is another kind of religion altogether.
—Neil Postman
(Discipleship, Discipline)

Jesus promised his disciples three things: that they would be entirely fearless, absurdly happy, and that they would get into trouble.
—W. Russell Maltby
(Discipleship, Peace)

Most of us spend the first six days of each week sowing wild oats; then we go to church on Sunday and pray for a crop failure.
—Fred Allen
(Sin, Rebellion)

Church

Let none pretend that they love the brethren in general,
and love the people of God, and love the saints, while
their love is not fervently exercised towards those who
are in the same church society with them. Christ will try
your love at the last day by your deportment in that
church wherein you are.
—John Owen
(Love, Judgment)

The church should be a community of dates instead of
pumpkins. Pumpkins you can harvest in six months.
Dates have to be planted and tended by people who will
not live to harvest them. Dates are for future genera-
tions.
—George Chauncey
(Patience, Maturity)

It is not the business of the church to adapt Christ to
men, but men to Christ.
—Dorothy Sayers
(Christ, Change)

Away with those who want an entirely pure church!
That is plainly the same thing as wanting no church at
all.
—Martin Luther
(Purity, Acceptance)

The first two laws of the church: (1) When other people
have abandoned something, we discover it; (2) When
people discover something wonderful that we have, we
have just abandoned it.
—Andrew Greeley
(Culture, Discovery)

The church must be reminded that it is not the master or the servant of the state, but rather the conscience of the state.   —Martin Luther King, Jr.
(Politics, Conscience)

The church is the glue that keeps us together when we disagree. It is the gasoline that keeps us going during the tough times. It is the guts that enables us to take risks when we need to.   —Mary Nelson
(Community, Courage)

The church is the only cooperative society in the world that exists for the benefit of its nonmembers.
—William Temple
(Evangelism, Outreach)

Anyone can love the ideal church. The challenge is to love the real church.   —Bishop Joseph McKinney
(Idealism, Love)

It is of no avail to talk of the church in general, the church in the abstract, unless the concrete particular local church which the people attend can become a center of light and leading, of inspiration and guidance, for its specific community.   —Rufus Jones
(Idealism, Community)

It was one of the Wesleys, I think, who said that the New Testament knows nothing of solitary religion. We are forbidden to neglect the assembling of ourselves together. Christianity is already institutional in the earliest of its documents.
—C. S. Lewis
(Fellowship, Christianity)

We don't live alone. We are members of one body. We are responsible for each other. And I tell you that the time will soon come when, if men will not learn that lesson, then they will be taught it in fire and blood and anguish.
—J. B. Priestley
(Community, Responsibility)

Church Growth

I have not followed a secret formula in the mighty church growth we are experiencing. There is no question in my mind that what has been done in Korea can also be duplicated in every part of the world. The key is prayer!
—David Yonggi Cho
(Evangelism, Prayer)

Commitment

In our modern world, our real danger comes not from irreligion, but from mild religion.
—D. Elton Trueblood
(Lukewarmness, Conviction)

You will invest your life in something, or you will throw it away on nothing.
—Haddon Robinson
(Investment, Waste)

Community

A community is only a community when the majority of its members are making the transition from "the community for myself" to "myself for the community."
—Jean Vanier
(Church, Fellowship)

The Bible is all about community: from the Garden of Eden to the City at the end. —George F. MacLeod
(Church, Fellowship)

If we don't accept Jesus in one another, we will not be able to give him to others. —Mother Teresa
(Acceptance, Jesus)

It takes a village to raise a child.
—African proverb
(Fellowship, Children)

Compassion

Warmth, warmth, more warmth! For we are dying of cold and not of darkness. It is not the night that kills, but the frost. —Miguel DeUnamuno
(Apathy, Coldness)

Let my heart be broken by the things that break the heart of God. —Bob Pierce
(God, Heart)

Compromise

The swift wind of compromise is a lot more devastating than the sudden jolt of misfortune. —Charles Swindoll
(Misfortune, Commitment)

27

Condemnation

It's worth noting that Jesus didn't condemn bad people. He condemned "stiff" people. We condemn the bad ones and affirm the stiff ones.

—Steve Brown
(Compassion, Acceptance)

Confession

We need not "sin that grace may abound." We *are* sinners and need only to confess that grace may abound.

—C. FitzSimons Allison
(Sin, Grace)

Conflict

If two people agree on everything, you may be sure that one of them is doing all the thinking.

—Anonymous
(Agreement, Thinking)

Figure out what went wrong, not who was wrong, when communication breaks down.

—Tom Nash
(Communication, Blame)

The secret of every discord in Christian homes and communities and churches is that we seek our own way and our own glory.

—Alan Redpath
(Home, Community)

Conscience

There is only one way to achieve happiness on this terrestrial ball. And that is to have either a clear conscience or none at all.

—Ogden Nash
(Happiness, Guilt)

Contentment

Next to faith this is the highest art—to be content with
the calling in which God has placed you. I have not
learned it yet. —Martin Luther
(Calling, Faith)

One who makes it a rule to be content in every part and
accident of life because it comes from God praises God
in a much higher manner than one who has some set
time for the singing of psalms. —William Law
(Praise, Acceptance)

Give a man everything he desires and yet at this very
moment he will feel that everything is not everything.
—Immanuel Kant
(Desire, Satisfaction)

A man looking at the present in light of the future, and
taking his whole being into account, may be contented
with his lot: that is Christian contentment. But if a man
has come to that point where he is so content that he
says "I do not want to know any more, or do any more,
or be any more," he is in a state in which he ought to be
changed into a mummy. —Henry Ward Beecher
(Growth, Knowledge)

It is right to be contented with what we have, never
with what we are. —James Mackintosh
(Growth, Character)

Contentment consists not in adding more fuel, but in taking away some fire; not in multiplying of wealth, but in subtracting our desires.
—Thomas Fuller
(Desire, Wealth)

Control
Dear God, I find it so easy to try to be the one in charge. I find it so painful to realize that I am not the one in control. Help me know when saying "I just work here" that it is a confession and not just a way of evading responsibility.
—Dick Rasanen
(Prayer, Submission)

Conversion
Conversion is not implanting eyes, for they exist already; but giving them direction, which they have not.
—Plato
(Vision, Direction)

My God, grant me the conversion of my parish; I am willing to suffer all my life whatsoever it may please thee to lay upon me; yes even for a hundred years am I prepared to endure the sharpest pains; only let my people be converted. My God, convert my parish.
—Cure d'Ars
(Church, Prayer)

Conviction
When you read God's word, you must constantly be saying to yourself, "It is talking to me, and about me."
—Soren Kierkegaard
(Word of God, Application)

In matters of style, swim with the current. In matters of
principle, stand like a rock. —Thomas Jefferson
(Principle, Style)

Too much of our orthodoxy is correct and sound, but
like words without a tune, it does not glow and burn; it
does not stir the heart; it has lost its hallelujah. One
man with a genuine glowing experience with God is
worth a library full of arguments. —Vance Havner
(Experience, Apologetics)

The Christian way is not the middle way between
extremes, but the narrow way between precipices.
—Donald Bloesch
(Extremes, Compromise)

Cooperation

What is most rewarding is doing something that really
matters with congenial colleagues who share with us
the firm conviction that it needs to be done.
—Elton Trueblood
(Community, Conviction)

Our world has become a neighborhood without becoming a brotherhood. —Billy Graham
(Community, Love)

Coping

Coping with difficult people is always a problem, espe-
cially if the difficult person happens to be yourself.
—Anonymous
(Self-awareness, Conflict)

31

Courage

Give us grace, O God, to do the deed which we well
know cries to be done. Let us not hesitate because of
ease, or the words of men's mouths, or our own lives.
Mighty causes are calling us . . . But they call with voices that mean work and sacrifice and death. Mercifully
grant us, O God, the spirit of Esther, that we say, "I will
go unto the King and if I perish, I perish." Amen.
—W. E. B. DuBois
(Conviction, Sacrifice)

Courage is being scared to death but saddling up any-
way.
—John Wayne
(Conviction, Sacrifice)

Courage is almost a contradiction in terms. It means a
strong desire to live taking the form of a readiness to
die.
—G.K. Chesterton
(Life, Death)

I am in earnest; I will not equivocate; I will not excuse; I
will not retreat a single inch; and I will be heard.
—William Lloyd Garrison
Nineteenth-century abolitionist
(Social Protest, Speech)

Courage! I have shown it for years; think you I shall
lose it at the moment when my sufferings are to end?
—Marie Antoinette
(Suffering, Strength)

Courtesy

The test of good manners is to be able to put up pleasantly with bad ones.
—Wendell Willkie

(Self-control, Conflict)

Covetousness

Covetousness is simply craving more of what you have enough of already.
—Haddon Robinson

(Desire, Wealth)

Envy is thin because it bites but never eats.
—Spanish proverb

(Envy, Gossip)

Creation

A number of materialistic thinkers have ascribed to blind evolution more miracles, more improbable coincidences and wonders, than all the teleologists could ever devise.
—Isaac Bashevis Singer

(Evolution, Materialism)

If man is not a divinity, then man is a disease. Either he is the image of God or else he is the one animal which has gone mad.
—G. K. Chesterton

(Human Nature, God's Image)

The sky is the daily bread of the eyes.
—Ralph Waldo Emerson

(Beauty, Nature)

Spring is God's way of saying, "One more time!"
—Robert Orben
(Nature, Seasons)

Creativity
What is there left in the world for original dissertation research?
—Doctoral student at Princeton, 1952
(Learning, Education)

Credibility
The *how* of being people worth listening to is by letting our lives be filled with God himself. The *why* of being people worth listening to is because we are his, and he wants us to radiate him.
—Carole Mayhall
(Character, Holy Spirit)

Crisis
Circumstances may appear to wreck our lives and God's plans, but God is not helpless among the ruins. Our broken lives are not lost or useless. God comes in and takes the calamity and uses it victoriously, working out his wonderful plan of love.
—Eric Liddell
(Sovereignty, God's Plan)

Criticism
People ask you for criticism, but they only want praise.
—W. Somerset Maugham
(Praise, Honesty)

Whatever you have to say to people, be sure to say it in words that will cause them to smile and you will be on pretty safe ground. And when you do find it necessary to criticize someone, put your criticism in the form of a question which the other fellow is practically sure to have to answer in a manner that he becomes his own critic.
—John Wanamaker
(Speech, Discipleship)

Great spirits have always encountered violent opposition from mediocre minds.
—Albert Einstein
(Opposition, Greatness)

The porcupine, whom we must handle gloved, may be respected, but is never loved.
—Arthur Guiterman
(Love, Respect)

Criticism should not be querulous and wasting, all knife and root-puller, but guiding, instructive, inspiring—a south wind, not an east wind.
—Ralph Waldo Emerson
(Gentleness, Discipleship)

The angry word is a blow struck at our brother, a stab at his heart: it seeks to hit, to hurt, and to destroy. A deliberate insult is worse, for we openly disgrace our brother in the eyes of the world, causing others to despise him.
—Dietrich Bonhoeffer
(Anger, Insult)

If one man calls you a donkey, pay him no mind. If two men call you a donkey, look for hoofprints. If three call you a donkey, get a saddle.
—Unknown
(Accountability, Listening)

35

Get your friends to tell you your faults, or better still, welcome an enemy who will watch you keenly and sting you savagely. What a blessing such an irritating critic will be to a wise man, what an intolerable nuisance to a fool!

—Charles Spurgeon
(Accountability, Enemies)

I would rather be disagreed with by someone who understands me, than to be agreed with by someone who does not understand me.

—James D. Glasse
(Agreement, Understanding)

The defects of a preacher are soon spied. Let him be endowed with ten virtues and have but one fault, and that one fault will eclipse and darken all his virtues and gifts, so evil is the world in these times.

—Martin Luther
(Gossip, Preaching)

To avoid criticism, say nothing, do nothing, be nothing.

—Fred Shero
(Courage, Leadership)

Cross

If thou bear the cross cheerfully, it will bear thee.

—Thomas a Kempis
(Cheerfulness, Suffering)

This only we may be assured of, that if tomorrow brings a cross, He who sends it can and will send grace to bear it.

—J. C. Ryle
(Grace, Assurance)

My wife is . . . a mirror. When I have sinned against her, my sin appears in the suffering of her face. . . . The passion of Christ . . . is such a mirror. Are the tears of my dear wife hard to look at? Well, the pain in the face of Jesus is harder. . . . Nevertheless, I will not avoid this mirror! No, I will carefully rehearse, again this year, the passion of my Jesus—with courage, with clarity and faith; for this is the mirror of dangerous grace, purging more purely than any other.

—Walter Wangerin, Jr.
(Grace, Sin)

The story we're called to tell and live and die by is one of risk confronted, death embraced. What's more, Jesus calls us to walk the narrow way, take up a cross with him, daily. It's terribly risky business. Ask that bright company of martyrs that quite recklessly parted with goods, security, and life itself, preferring to be faithful in death rather than safe in life.

—William H. Willimon
(Risk, Martyrdom)

[Jesus] rose up from the place where the kingdoms of the world shimmered before him, where crowns flashed and banners rustled, and hosts of enthusiastic people were ready to acclaim him, and quietly walked the way of poverty and suffering to the cross.

—Helmut Thielicke
(Suffering, Sacrifice)

37

If that was God on that cross, then the hill called Skull
is a granite studded with stakes to which you can
anchor.
—Max Lucado
(Trust, Good Friday)

It's easiest to see the cross on Jesus' shoulders. It's a bit
harder with our neighbor's cross. Most difficult of all is
seeing our own cross.
—Mieczyslaw Malinski
(Suffering, Responsibility)

Culture
There's a lot more money to be made on Wall Street. If
you want real power, go to Washington. If you want sex,
go into the fashion business. But if you want the whole
poison cocktail in one glass—go to Hollywood.
—Alec Baldwin, actor
(Money, Power, Sex)

Dostoyevsky reminded us in *The Brothers Karamazov*
that "if God does not exist, everything is permissible."
We are now seeing "everything." And much of it is not
good to get used to.
—William J. Bennett
(Sin, God)

The only effective response to our nation's crime prob-
lem is spiritual revival.
—N. Lee Cooper
President-elect of the
American Bar Association
(Crime, Revival)

Man creates culture and through culture creates himself.
—Pope John Paul II
(Influence, Sin)

We live in a strange society where we make documen-
taries of serial killers, movie idols out of organized
crime members, authors out of political crooks, and role
models out of criminals who beat the system . . . I don't
know when crime went from being news to entertainment, but somehow it's made the transition.
—Erma Bombeck
(Crime, Entertainment)

Cynicism
Cynicism has gone too far. We are becoming what the
history books tell us late Rome was like: mired in deca-
dent self-absorption and lacking virtue.
—Oliver Stone, movie director
(Decadence, Virtue)

Death

Why is it that we rejoice at a birth and grieve at a funeral? It is because we are not the person involved.

—Mark Twain
(Birth, Grief)

We come into this world with our fingers curled and only slowly, by repeated practice, do we learn to open our hands. It takes a great deal of dying to get us ready to live.

—Virginia Stem Owens
(Openness, Growth)

If you attempt to talk with a dying man about sports or business, he is no longer interested. He now sees other things as more important. People who are dying recognize what we often forget, that we are standing on the brink of another world.

—William Law
(Eternity, Priorities)

If you live wrong, you can't die right.

—Billy Sunday
(Righteousness, Life)

Deception

We can easily forgive a child who is afraid of the dark; the real tragedy of life is when men are afraid of the light.

—Plato
(Sin, Darkness)

An error is the more dangerous the more truth it contains.

—Henri-Frederic Amiel
(Truth, Danger)

Decisions

Ideally when Christians meet as Christians to take counsel together, their purpose is not—or should not be—to ascertain what is in the mind of the majority but what is in the mind of the Holy Spirit—something which may be quite different.

—Margaret Thatcher
(Church, Holy Spirit)

Depravity

I think it says something that the only form of life that we have created so far [computer viruses] is purely destructive. Talk about creating life in our own image.

—Stephen W. Hawking
(Human Nature, Creativity)

One of the enduring images in Christian culture is the praying hypocrite—the slave trader who reads the Bible in the hull of the ship; the preacher whose prayers bring him wealth; the convicted criminal who suddenly embraces religion. But don't we all have a bit of the hypocrite or con artist in us? Don't we all sometimes overlook our faults as we pray with the seemingly uninformed heart of a child? Prayer doesn't fail us; we fail prayer.
—Jay Copp
(Hypocrisy, Prayer)

Desire

We are disgusted by the things that we desire, and we desire what disgusts us.
—Mario Cuomo
(Disgust, Covetousness)

Destiny

Destiny is not a matter of chance; it is a matter of choice.
—William Jennings Bryan
(Choices, Chance)

Devil

The Devil is like a mad dog that is chained up. He is powerless to harm us when we are outside his reach, but once we enter his circle we expose ourselves again to injury or harm.
—Augustine
(Harm, Protection)

The Devil's most beautiful ruse is to convince us that he does not exist.
—Pierre Baudelaire
(Doubt, Deception)

Devotion

Keep us, Lord, so awake in the duties of our calling that
we may sleep in thy peace and wake in thy glory.
—John Donne
(Duty, Calling)

If life is to have meaning, and if God's will is to be done,
all of us have to accept who we are and what we are,
give it back to God, and thank him for the way he made
us. What I am is God's gift to me; what I do with it is
my gift to him.
—Warren W. Wiersbe
(Acceptance, Giving)

Devotional Life

How many Christians look upon it as a burden and a
duty and a difficulty to get alone with God! That is the
great hindrance to our Christian life everywhere.
—Andrew Murray
(Prayer, Duty)

The Word of God is demanding. It demands a stretch of
time in our day—even though it be a very modest one—
in which it is our *only* companion . . . God will not put
up with being fobbed off with prayers in telegram style
and cut short like a troublesome visitor for whom we
open the door just a crack to get rid of him as quickly as
possible.
—Helmut Thielicke
(Word of God, Time)

44

If you've made a habit of communing with God when the sun is shining, you'll find it much easier to sing in the rain.   —Bill Pannell
(God, Difficulty)

Difficulty

What we do in the crisis always depends on whether we see the difficulties in the light of God, or God in the shadow of the difficulties.   —G. Campbell Morgan
(Crisis, God)

Looking back, [my wife] Jan and I have learned that the wilderness is part of the landscape of faith, and every bit as essential as the mountaintop. On the mountaintop we are overwhelmed by God's presence. In the wilderness we are overwhelmed by his absence. Both places should bring us to our knees; the one, in utter awe; the other, in utter dependence.   —Dave Dravecky
(God, Faith)

Bad times have a scientific value. These are occasions a good learner would not miss.   —Ralph Waldo Emerson
(Learning, Suffering)

With me a change of trouble is as good as a vacation.
—David Lloyd George
(Change, Refreshment)

We are too little to be able always to rise above difficulties. Well, then, let us pass beneath them quite simply.
—Therese of Lisieux
(Humility, Perseverance)

The difficult we do immediately; the impossible takes a little longer.　　　　　　—U.S. Navy Seabees slogan, World War II
(Challenge, Teamwork)

Discernment

God never gives us discernment in order that we may criticize, but that we may intercede.

—Oswald Chambers
(Criticism, Intercession)

The great thing is to get the true picture, whatever it is.
—Winston Churchill
(Truth, Learning)

Reading God's hand into circumstances can be an evasion of genuine commitment to being his person in them. It can be an insidious alternative to giving Him your heart—because it keeps your attention directed outward rather than inward, where his chisel bites. . . . We have elevated coincidence to the status of miracle, and the interpretation of coincidence to gospel. We can routinely ask God to intervene in our circumstances while hoping he'll keep his nose out of inner things like our spiritual indifference and pride.　　　　—John Boykin
(Submission, Miracles)

Discipleship

Full-grown oaks are not produced in three years; neither are servants of God.　　　　　　　—Douglas Rumford
(Growth, Patience)

We teach what we know; we reproduce what we are.
—Robert Schmidgall
(Education, Change)

In a church in Verona stands, or rather sits, a wooden image of St. Zeno, an ancient bishop, with knees so ludicrously short that there is no lap on which a baby could be held. He was not the first nor the last ecclesiastic who has been utterly incapable of being a nursing father to the church. It would be good if all ministers had a heavenly instinct for the nourishing and bringing up of the Lord's little ones, but this quality is sadly lacking.
—Charles Spurgeon
(Compassion, Ministry)

Discipline

Liberty is the right to discipline ourselves in order not to be disciplined by others.
—Clemenceau
(Liberty, Self-control)

Discipline begets abundance. Abundance, unless we use utmost care, destroys discipline. Discipline in its fall pulls down with it abundance.
—Anonymous
(Abundance, Self-control)

Discipline is the refining fire by which talent becomes ability.
—Roy L. Smith
(Talent, Ability)

To live a disciplined life, and to accept the result of that discipline as the will of God—that is the mark of a man.
—Tom Landry
(Character, Manhood)

Discretion
Discretion is leaving a few things unsaid.
—Elbert Hubbard
(Tact, Speech)

Duty
The greatest thing is to be found at one's post as a child of God, living each day as though it were our last, but planning as though our world might last a hundred years.
—C. S. Lewis
(Planning, Responsibility)

Every generation is strategic. We are not responsible for the past generation, and we cannot bear full responsibility for the next one; but we do have our generation. God will hold us responsible as to how well we fulfill our responsibilities to this age and take advantage of our opportunities.
—Billy Graham
(Opportunity, Responsibility)

Many people neglect the task that lies at hand and are content with having wished to do the impossible.
—Teresa of Avila
(Neglect, Idealism)

Now my heart is troubled, and what shall I say? "Father, save me from this hour"? No, it was for this very reason I came to this hour.
—Jesus Christ (John 12:36)
(Dedication, Courage)

Easter

The preacher brings a report from the battlefield of the conflict between Christ and Satan. The news is that for the whole of humankind Jesus Christ has won the victory in his death and resurrection. —James W. Cox
(Spiritual Warfare, Resurrection)

When death stung Jesus Christ, it stung itself to death.
—Peter Joshua
(Death, Victory)

Easter suffers from acute holiday envy. Its egg hunts and rabbit have never had the commercial appeal of Santa's bounty and eight tiny reindeer. Let's face it, cattle lowing and a baby who doesn't cry is money in the bank compared to a homeless thirty-year-old dangling from a cross. —Joey Earl Horstmann
(Christmas, Cross)

I cannot give in to the Devil's principal, deceitful tactic which makes so many Christians satisfied with an "Easter celebration" instead of experiencing the power of Christ's resurrection. It is the Devil's business to keep Christians mourning and weeping with pity beside the cross instead of demonstrating that Jesus Christ is risen, indeed.
—A. W. Tozer
(Power, Resurrection)

Many think the Christian religion has run its course and that the gloom of Good Friday is now settling over the long history of the church. But they are wrong. The reality of the Resurrection cannot so easily be undone. In truth, it is the world of unbelievers that remains on notice of judgment.
—Carl F. H. Henry
(Resurrection, Judgment)

Ego
Arrogant, pompous, obnoxious, vain, cruel, verbose, a showoff. I have been called all of these. Of course, I am.
—Howard Cosell
(Pride, Self-evaluation)

Emotion
If choice must be made between rationality and fervor, men will choose fervor.
—George A. Buttrick
(Rationalism, Enthusiasm)

Encouragement

A pat on the back is only a few vertebrae removed from a kick in the pants, but is miles ahead in results.

—Ella Wheeler Wilcox
(Motivation, Criticism)

Enemies

Friends may come and go, but enemies accumulate.

—David Belasic
(Friendship, Criticism)

Envy

The man who keeps busy helping the man below him won't have time to envy the man above him.

—Henrietta Mears
(Service, Contentment)

Eternal Life

Nations, cultures, arts, civilizations—these are mortal, and their life is to ours as the life of a gnat. But it is immortals whom we joke with, work with, marry, snub, and exploit—immortal horrors or everlasting splendors.

—C. S. Lewis
(Human Nature, Immortality)

We take excellent care of our bodies, which we have for only a lifetime; yet we shrivel our souls, which we will have for eternity.

—Billy Graham
(Soul, Body)

Ethics

The world has achieved brilliance without conscience.
Ours is a world of nuclear giants and ethical infants.
—Omar Bradley
(Conscience, Progress)

The church is uncommonly vocal about the subject of
bedrooms and so singularly silent on the subject of
boardrooms!
—Dorothy L. Sayers
(Leadership, Unity)

Evangelism

Saving knowledge is diffused over the earth, not like
sunlight but like torchlight, which is passed from hand
to hand.
—James Strachan
(Witness, Relationships)

I would rather fail in the cause that some day will tri-
umph than triumph in a cause that some day will fail.
—Woodrow Wilson
(Missions, Church)

There is a subtle false teaching that says we can be
evangelical without being evangelistic. It has us believe
we "go" to church rather than we "are" the church.
—Chris A. Lyons
(Church, Missions)

The church that does not evangelize will fossilize.
—Oswald J. Smith
(Church, Apathy)

The gospel is good news only if it arrives in time.
—Carl F. H. Henry
(Gospel, Time)

I feel that God has put me beside a cliff where people
dance close to the edge. I say to them, "Look, if I were
you I wouldn't get so close. I have seen people go over,
and they always get hurt. Some of them get killed."
And they say, "I really appreciate your telling me that. I
didn't realize it was so dangerous." And then they jump!
I feel so responsible for the pain. And the Father
reminds me through his Word, "Son, you are not responsible for the jumping; you are responsible for the telling.
As long as you are faithful, you don't have to play God."
—Steve Brown
(Responsibility, Choices)

It is our privilege to have world evangelism as a passion,
not our responsibility to have as a burden.
—Mary Nordstrom
(Passion, Burden)

The world has more winnable people than ever
before . . . but it is possible to come out of a ripe field
empty-handed.
—Donald McGavran
(Missions, Opportunity)

The gospel must be preached afresh and told in new
ways to every generation, since every generation has its
own unique questions. The gospel must constantly be
forwarded to a new address, because the recipient is
repeatedly changing his place of residence.
—Helmut Thielicke
(Gospel, Creativity)

The idea is not to get the word out, but to let the Word
out.
—Dick Rasanen
(Witness, Word of God)

Consumers want to know not only what they're buying,
but *who* they're buying it from. . . . Consumer relationship development is as important as product development.
—Frank P. Perdue
(Witness, Relationships)

It could be that one of the greatest hindrances to evange-
lism today is the poverty of our own experience.
—Billy Graham
(Experience, Hypocrisy)

Evil

Once we assuage our conscience by calling something a
"necessary evil," it begins to look more and more necessary and less and less evil.
—Sydney J. Harris
(Conscience, Deception)

Why did Jesus Christ not remain alive and eliminate,
generation by generation, all the evils which harass
humanity? Simply because he was the Great Physician,
and in the finest tradition of medical science, he was
unwilling to remain preoccupied with the symptoms
when he could destroy the disease. Jesus Christ was
unwilling to settle for anything less than elimination of
the cause of all evil in history.
—Richard C. Halverson
(Christ, Cross)

Men never do evil so completely and cheerfully as when they do it from religious conviction. —Blaise Pascal
(Religion, Conviction)

When a man is getting better, he understands more and more clearly the evil that is still left in him. When a man is getting worse, he understands his own badness less and less. —C. S. Lewis
(Self-deception, Good)

Example
God has no more precious gift to a church or an age than a man who lives as an embodiment of his will, and inspires those around him with the faith of what grace can do. —Andrew Murray
(Grace, Inspiration)

Excellence
The society which scorns excellence in plumbing because plumbing is a humble activity, and tolerates shoddiness in philosophy because it is an exalted activity, will have neither good plumbing nor good philosophy. Neither its pipes nor its theories will hold water. —John Gardner
(Shoddiness, Tolerance)

Badness you can get easily, in quantity: the road is smooth and lies close by. But in front of excellence the immortal gods have put sweat, and long and steep is the way to it, and rough at first. But when you come to the top, then it is easy, even though it is hard.

—Hesiod
(Difficulty, Work)

Excuses

Never excuse. Never explain. Never complain.
—Motto of the British Foreign Service
(Leadership, Character)

Expectations

Treat a man as he appears to be, and you make him worse. But treat a man as if he already were what he potentially could be, and you make him what he should be.

—Johann Wolfgang Goethe
(Growth, Motivation)

Attempt great things for God. Expect great things from God.

—William Carey
(Ambition, Motivation)

It is a fundamental principle in the life and walk of faith that we must always be prepared for the unexpected when we are dealing with God.

—D. Martyn Lloyd-Jones
(Sovereignity, Trials)

I always prefer to believe the best of everybody—it saves so much trouble.

—Rudyard Kipling
(Church, Community)

Failure

We fight for lost causes because we know that our
defeat and dismay may be the preface for our successor's victory.   —T. S. Eliot
                                      (Causes, Victory)

One reason God created time was so there would be a
place to bury the failures of the past.   —James Long
                                           (Time, Past)

Take away my ability to fail and I would not know the
meaning of success. Let me be immune to rejection and
heartbreak and I could not know the glory of living.
                                           —Ross W. Marrs
                                          (Success, Pain)

I cannot give you the formula for success, but I can give
you the formula for failure, which is: Try to please
everybody.   —Herbert Bayard Swope
                                   (Success, Peer Pressure)

The increase of suicides, alcoholics, and even some forms of nervous breakdowns is evidence that many people are training for success when they should be training for failure. Failure is far more common than success; poverty is more prevalent than wealth, and disappointment more normal than arrival.

—J. Wallace Hamilton
(Success, Perseverance)

Whenever you fall, pick up something.

—Oswald Avery
(Learning, Growth)

We never see God in failure, but only in success—a strange attitude for people who have the cross as the center of their faith.

—Cheryl Forbes
(Success, Cross)

A moment of conscious triumph makes one feel that after this nothing will really matter; a moment of realized disaster makes one feel that this is the end of everything. But neither feeling is realistic, for neither event is really what it is felt to be.

—J. I. Packer
(Success, Perspective)

Faith

Faith like Job's cannot be shaken because it is the result of having been shaken.

—Abraham Heschel
(Certainty, Difficulty)

What else will do *except* faith in such a cynical, corrupt time? When the country goes temporarily to the dogs, cats must learn to be circumspect, walk on fences, sleep in trees, and have faith that all this woofing is not the last word.
—Garrison Keillor
(Cynicism, World)

A weak faith is weakened by predicaments and catastrophes whereas a strong faith is strengthened by them.
—Victor Frankl
(Trials, Strength)

Jesus holds the answers to all of the everyday problems that you face. I am talking about an acceptance and belief in Jesus, heaven, and God. I guess you can deal with your problems on your own without these beliefs, but it's much, much tougher. With those beliefs, you realize how insignificant the budget deficit debate is in comparison with the big picture.
—Rush Limbaugh
(Jesus, Problems)

Faith means trusting in advance what will only make sense in reverse.
—Philip Yancey
(Vision, Trust)

Faith must never be counter to reason; yet it must always go beyond reason, for the nature of man is more than rationalism. Faith is emotion as well as reason.
—George A. Buttrick
(Reason, Emotion)

That you are sitting before me in this church is a fact. That I am standing and speaking to you from this pulpit is a fact. But it is only faith that makes me believe anyone is listening.
—Anonymous preacher
(Fact, Belief)

Faith is not belief without proof but trust without reservation.
—Elton Trueblood
(Trust, Belief)

It is a fatal error to mistake mere historical belief for saving faith. A man may firmly believe his religion historically, and yet have no part nor portion therein practically and savingly. He must not only believe his faith, he must believe *in* his faith.
—Thomas More
(Belief, Religion)

True faith goes into operation when there are no answers.
—Elisabeth Elliot
(Difficulty, Doubt)

Faith does not operate in the realm of the possible. There is no glory for God in that which is humanly possible. Faith begins where man's power ends.
—George Müller
(Power, Glory)

Our faith becomes practical when it is expressed in two books: the date book and the check book.
—Elton Trueblood
(Time, Money)

Hope is hearing the melody of the future. Faith is to dance to it.
—Rubem Alves
(Hope, Future)

I prayed for faith, and thought that some day faith would come down and strike me like lightning. But faith did not seem to come. One day I read in the tenth chapter of Romans, "Now faith cometh by hearing, and hearing by the Word of God." I had closed my Bible, and prayed for faith. I now opened my Bible, and began to study, and faith has been growing ever since.
—D. L. Moody
(Bible, Study)

Faith is to believe what we do not see, and the reward of this faith is to see what we believe.
—Augustine
(Vision, Belief)

Nothing worth doing is completed in one lifetime: therefore we must be saved by hope. Nothing true or beautiful makes complete sense in any context of history: therefore we must be saved by faith. Nothing we do, no matter how virtuous, can be accomplished alone: therefore we are saved by love.
—Reinhold Niebuhr
(Hope, Love)

False Teachers

False teachers invite people to come to the Master's table because of what's on it, not because they love the Master.
—Hank Hanegraaff
(Leadership, Teaching)

Fame

Don't confuse fame with success. Madonna is one, and
Helen Keller is the other.   —Erma Bombeck
(Success, Character)

The fame of great men should always be judged by the
methods they employed to achieve it.
                          —Francois de la Rochefoucauld
                               (Character, Achievement)

Family

Abraham was chosen to be a blessing to the whole
earth, but his vocation was to begin to take effect in the
simplest way. He was called to teach his own house-
hold, who again would hand down the truth to their
households. His being a blessing to the world depended
on his being a blessing to his own home.
                                      —James Strachan
                                      (Blessing, Home)

The Christian home is the Master's workshop where the
processes of character molding are silently, lovingly,
faithfully, and successfully carried on.
                                       —Lord Houghton
                                      (Character, Home)

The tragedy of my life is that although I've led thousands of people to Jesus Christ, my own sons are not
saved.   —Billy Sunday
                                  (Children, Salvation)

Fanaticism
A fanatic is a person who can't change his mind and
won't change the subject.
—Winston Churchill
(Conviction, Change)

Our trouble with earnestness is that those who are pos-
sessed by it so often take it as proof certain that they are
on God's side.
—Eliot Porter
(Conviction, Humility)

Fatalism
I'm not a fatalist. And even if I were, what could I do
about it?
—Emo Philips
(Will, Freedom)

Fatherhood of God
We want, in fact, not so much a Father in heaven as a
grandfather in heaven—a senile benevolence who, as
they say, "liked to see young people enjoying themselves" and whose plan for the universe was simply that
it might be truly said at the end of each day, "a good
time was had by all."
—J. B. Phillips
(Theology, Indulgence)

Faultfinding
The initial temptation to try and fill one's predecessor's
shoes is soon followed by another—the temptation to fill
them with clay.
—Dick Rasanen
(Criticism, Envy)

Fear

Not to fear is the armor.

—Ulrich Zwingli
(Courage, Protection)

No one loves the man whom he fears.

—Aristotle
(Love, Relationships)

Fear knocked at the door. Faith answered. No one was there.

—Unknown
(Faith, Courage)

Fear of God

Erase all thought and fear of God from a community, and selfishness and sensuality would trample in scorn on the restraints of human laws. Virtue, duty, and principle would be mocked as unmeaning sounds.

—William Ellery Channing
(Selfishness, Virtue)

The remarkable thing about fearing God is that when you fear God you fear nothing else, whereas if you do not fear God you fear everything else.

—Oswald Chambers
(Courage, Devotion)

Fellowship

People join churches more because they want warmth than light. . . . Sermons may get them into church the first time, but what keeps them coming are friendships that foster inward awareness and support.

—Jack R. Van Ens
(Church, Friendship)

Flattery

Flattery, provided that it be disguised as something other than flattery, is infinitely sweet. So Brutus says of Caesar: "But when I tell him he hates flatterers, he says he does, being then most flattered."

—Richard John Neuhaus
(Deception, Motivation)

Forgiveness

The wonder of forgiveness has become a banality. It can be the death of our faith if we forget that it is literally a miracle.

—Helmut Thielicke
(Miracles, Faith)

What I envy most about you Christians is your forgiveness; I have nobody to forgive me.

—Marghanita Laski
Secular humanist and novelist,
before her death in 1988
(Witness, Guilt)

We pardon in the degree that we love.

—Francois de la Rochefoucauld
(Love, Pardon)

Free Will

If there are a thousand steps between us and God, he will take all but one. He will leave the final one for us. The choice is ours.

—Max Lucado
(Evangelism, Salvation)

Freedom

I have on my table a violin string. It is free. I twist one end of it and it responds. It is free. But it is not free to do what a violin string is supposed to do—to produce music. So I take it, fix it in my violin, and tighten it until it is taut. Only then is it free to be a violin string.

—Sir Rabindranath Tagore
(Self-restraint, Duty)

Friendship

Oh, the inexpressible comfort of feeling safe with a person; having neither to weigh thoughts nor measure words, but to pour them all out, just as they are, chaff and grain together, knowing that a faithful hand will take and sift them, keep what is worth keeping, and then, with the breath of kindness, blow the rest away.

—George Eliot
(Listening, Kindness)

We love those who know the worst of us and don't turn their faces away.

—Walker Percy
(Love, Devotion)

Future

We should all be concerned about the future because we will have to spend the rest of our lives there.

—Charles F. Kettering
(Concern, Life)

G

Gifts

God does not require that each individual shall have
capacity for everything.   —Richard Rothe
(Limitations, Acceptance)

I have known projects abandoned for lack of funds, but
not for lack of the gifts of the Spirit. Provided the human
resources are adequate we take the spiritual for granted.
                                                  —John V. Taylor
(Holy Spirit, Self-reliance)

Giving

You give but little when you give of your possessions. It
is when you give of yourself that you truly give.
                                                  —Kahlil Gibran
(Possessions, Stewardship)

Glory

God is looking for men in whose hands his glory is safe.
—A. W. Tozer
(God, Humility)

Resolved: that all men should live for the glory of God.
Resolved second: that whether others do or not, I will.
—Jonathan Edwards
(Determination, Purpose)

Your great glory is not to be inferior to what God has made you.
—Pericles
(Acceptance, Gifts)

God

If God exists, everything is possible; if there is no God, everything is permitted.
—Fyodor Dostoyevsky
(Sin, Possibilities)

One can be a good Jew, or a good Christian, with God or against God, but not without God.
—Elie Wiesel
(God's Presence, Faith)

God's might to direct me
God's power to protect me
God's wisdom for learning
God's eye for discerning
God's ear for my hearing
God's Word for my clearing.

—Saint Patrick
(Word of God, Power)

If you can explain what God is doing in your ministry, then God is not really in it. —Warren Wiersbe
(Ministry, Understanding)

To know and to serve God, of course, is why we're here, a clear truth that, like the nose on your face, is near at hand and easily discernible but can make you dizzy if you try to focus on it hard. But a little faith will see you through. —Garrison Keillor
(Knowledge, Service)

Let us think often that our only business in this life is to please God. —Brother Lawrence
(Discipleship, Devotion)

God's Knowledge

Nothing will more quickly rid us of laziness and coldness, of hypocrisy, cowardice, and pride than the knowledge that God sees, hears, and takes account. —John R. W. Stott
(Motivation, Sin)

Though you are one of the teeming millions in this world, and though the world would have you believe that you do not count and that you are but a speck in the mass, God says, "I know you." —D. Martyn Lloyd-Jones
(Value, Worth)

God's Will

O Lord, grant that I may do thy will as if it were my
will; so that thou mayest do my will as if it were thy
will.   —Augustine
                              (Obedience, Surrender)

Never confuse the will of the majority with the will of
God.   —Charles Colson
                             (Peer Pressure, Obedience)

To what are we to be consecrated? Not to Christian
work, but to the will of God, to be and to do whatever
he requires.   —Watchman Nee
                                (Ministry, Obedience)

I have found that the most extravagant dreams of boy-
hood have not surpassed the great experience of being
in the will of God, and I believe that nothing could be
better.   —Jim Elliot
                               (Reward, Satisfaction)

Spread out your petition before God, and then say, "Thy
will, not mine, be done." The sweetest lesson I have
learned in God's school is to let the Lord choose for me.
                                         —D. L. Moody
                               (Prayer, Sovereignty)

I believe the will of God prevails; without him all
human reliance is vain; without the assistance of that
Divine Being I cannot succeed; with that assistance I
cannot fail.   —Abraham Lincoln
                              (Self-reliance, Success)

Four questions a Christian might ask when making a career decision: (1) Is this a realistic opportunity? (2) Am I reasonably prepared to meet the challenge? (3) What is the counsel of godly men I respect? (4) What is the leading of the Holy Spirit? —Ed MacAteer
(Guidance, Decisions)

God's Work
To have God do his own work through us, even once, is better than a lifetime of human striving.
—Watchman Nee
(Sovereignty, Submission)

I used to ask God to help me. Then I asked if I might help him. I ended up asking him to do his work through me. —J. Hudson Taylor
(Service, Ministry)

God's Wrath
God's wrath is his utter intolerance of whatever degrades and destroys. He hates iniquity as a mother hates the polio that would take the life of the child.
—A. W. Tozer
(Sin, Holiness)

Good Works
We can't save ourselves by pulling on our bootstraps, even when the bootstraps are made of the finest religious leather. —Eugene Peterson
(Salvation, Self-reliance)

71

Do all the good you can,
By all the means you can,
In all the ways you can,
In all the places you can,
At all the times you can,
To all the people you can,
As long as ever you can.

—John Wesley
(Service, Missions)

The person who looks for quick results in the seed planting of well-doing will be disappointed. If I want potatoes for dinner tomorrow, it will do me little good to plant them in my garden tonight. There are long stretches of darkness and invisibility and silence that separate planting and reaping.

—Eugene Peterson
(Patience, Results)

A do-gooder is a person trying to live beyond his spiritual income.

—H. A. Williams
(Character, Maturity)

Gospel

The Resurrection is not only the Good News, it is the best news imaginable.

—Ray C. Stedman
(Resurrection, Easter)

Gossip

One of the striking differences between a cat and a lie is a cat only has nine lives.

—Mark Twain
(Truth, Lying)

Loose lips sink ships.
—World War II poster
(Speech, Self-control)

It takes two years to learn to talk and seventy years to learn to control your mouth.
—Unknown
(Speech, Truth)

Government
Just be glad you're not getting all the government you're paying for.
—Will Rogers
(Politics, Corruption)

The whole art of government consists in being honest.
—Thomas Jefferson
(Honesty, Leadership)

Grace
Those who would avoid the despair of sinfulness by staying far from God find they have also missed the forgiving grace of God.
—Charles E. Wolfe
(Sin, Forgiveness)

Cheap grace is the grace we bestow on ourselves. Cheap grace is the preaching of forgiveness without requiring repentance, baptism without church discipline, Communion without confession. Cheap grace is grace without discipleship, grace without the cross, grace without Jesus Christ, living and incarnate.
—Dietrich Bonhoeffer
(Repentance, Discipline)

Remember the great need you have of the grace and assistance of God. You should never lose sight of him—not for a moment.
—Andrew Murray
(God, Vision)

Saving grace makes a man as willing to leave his lusts as a slave is willing to leave his galley, or a prisoner his dungeon, or a thief his bolts, or a beggar his rags.
—Thomas Brooks
(Repentance, Change)

Greatness

It is a rough road that leads to the heights of greatness.
—Seneca
(Trials, Character)

Those who aim at great deeds must also suffer greatly.
—Plutarch
(Suffering, Achievement)

Growth

Growth for the sake of growth is the ideology of the cancer cell.
—Edward Abbey
(Maturity, Evangelism)

If you have the Spirit without the Word, you blow up. If you have the Word without the Spirit, you dry up. If you have both the Word and the Spirit, you grow up.
—Don Lyon
(Holy Spirit, Word of God)

The Christian walk is much like riding a bicycle; we are either moving forward or falling off.
—Robert Tuttle
(Progress, Backsliding)

Guilt

I find it impossible to avoid offending guilty men, for there is no way of avoiding it but by our silence or their patience; and silent we cannot be because of God's command, and patient they cannot be because of their guilt.

—Martin Luther
(Truth, Conviction)

Happiness

The grand essentials of happiness are: something to do, something to love, and something to hope for.
—Thomas Chalmers
(Purpose, Hope)

When one door of happiness closes, another opens; but often we look so long at the closed door that we do not see the one which has been opened for us.
—Helen Keller
(Faith, Perspective)

There are three kinds of people: those who have sought God and found him, and these are reasonable and happy; those who seek God and have not yet found him, and these are reasonable and unhappy; and those who neither seek God nor find him, and these are unreasonable and unhappy.
—Blaise Pascal
(God, Satisfaction)

If your happiness (or health) depends on what some-
body else says (or does), I guess you do have a problem.
—Richard Bach
(Acceptance, Peer Pressure)

I think we have lost the old knowledge that happiness is
overrated. . . . Our ancestors believed in two worlds, and
understood this to be the solitary, poor, nasty, brutish,
and short one. We are the first generation of man that
actually expected to find happiness here on earth, and
our search for it has caused such unhappiness.
—Peggy Noonan
(Eternity, Contentment)

Feeling better has become more important to us than
finding God.
—Larry Crabb
(Feelings, Faith)

Hatred

Hate is born when men call evil good. And like an
infant serpent bursting from its small, confining shell, it
can never be cased so small again.
—Calvin Miller
(Evil, Sin)

I hate everybody. I know they say, "Now, you can't hate
the world; don't be bitter." But I just hate everybody.
—Heavyweight boxer Mike Tyson
(Bitterness, Anger)

Heart

Out in front of us is the drama of men and of nations, seething, struggling, laboring, dying . . . but within the silences of the souls of men an eternal drama is ever being enacted. . . . On the outcome of this inner drama rests, ultimately, the outer pageant of history.

—Thomas Kelly
(Eternity, Purpose)

Heaven

The great thing in this world is not so much where we stand as in what direction we are moving. To reach the port of heaven, we must sail sometimes with the wind and sometimes against it—but we must sail, and not drift, nor lie at anchor.

—Oliver Wendell Holmes
(Progress, Eternity)

We are afraid that heaven is a bribe, and that if we make it our goal we shall no longer be disinterested. It is not so. Heaven offers nothing that a mercenary soul can desire. It is safe to tell the pure in heart that they shall see God, for only the pure in heart want to.

—C. S. Lewis
(Eternity, Hope)

We see heaven more clearly through the prism of tears.

—Robertson McQuilken
(Sorrow, Eternity)

Hell

The one principle of hell is "I am my own!"

—George MacDonald
(Self-reliance, Pride)

The mind is its own place, and in itself
Can make a Heav'n of Hell, a Hell of Heav'n.
—John Milton
(Heaven, Mind)

Heroism
True heroism is remarkably sober, very undramatic. It is
not the urge to surpass all others at whatever cost, but the
urge to serve others at whatever cost. —Arthur Ashe
(Service, Sacrifice)

Being positive is part of being a hero—maybe the hardest part, because if you are a hero you're smart enough
to know all the reasons why you should be discouraged.
—Michael Dorris
(Optimism, Discouragement)

Holiness
Am I becoming more and more in love with God as a
holy God, or with the conception of an amiable being
who says, "Oh, well, sin doesn't matter much"?
—Oswald Chambers
(God, Sin)

In our age, as in every age, people are longing for happiness, not realizing that what they are looking for is holiness. —Jerry L. Walls
(Happiness, Longing)

Some people get so caught up in their own holiness that
they look at the Trinity for a possible vacancy.
—John MacArthur
(Self-righteousness, Pride)

The world and the Cross do not get along too well
together, and comfort and holiness do not share the
same room. —Carlo Carretto
(Discipleship, Sacrifice)

All the holy men seem to have gone off and died.
There's no one left but us sinners to carry on the min-
istry. —Jamie Buckingham
(Discipleship, Service)

Holy Spirit

We have given too much attention to methods and to
machinery and to resources, and too little to the Source
of Power, the filling with the Holy Ghost.
—J. Hudson Taylor
(Power, Unction)

Nothing is more dangerous than to put a wedge between
the Word and the Spirit, to emphasize either one at the
expense of the other. It is the Spirit and the Word, the
Spirit upon the Word, and the Spirit in us as we read the
Word. —D. Martyn Lloyd-Jones
(Word of God, Bible)

The church wants not more consecrated philanthropists,
but a disciplined priesthood of theocentric souls who
shall be tools and channels of the Spirit of God.
—Evelyn Underhill
(Stewardship, Obedience)

I have a glove here in my hand. The glove cannot do anything by itself, but when my hand is in it, it can do many things. True, it is not the glove, but my hand in the glove that acts.

We are gloves. It is the Holy Spirit in us who is the hand, who does the job. We have to make room for the hand so that every finger is filled. —Corrie Ten Boom
(Obedience, Sanctification)

Every time we say, "I believe in the Holy Spirit," we mean that we believe that there is a living God able and willing to enter human personality and change it.
—J. B. Phillips
(Change, Faith)

Home
Home is where people go when they're tired of being nice. —Anonymous
(Family, Relationships)

Honesty
To be persuasive, we must be believable. To be believable, we must be credible. To be credible, we must be truthful. —Edward R. Murrow
(Credibility, Truth)

Do not expect God to cover what you are not willing to uncover. —Duncan Campbell
(Confession, Truth)

If we are honest, we must admit that much of our time is spent pretending. But when we turn to God in prayer, we must present our real selves, candidly acknowledging our strengths and weaknesses and our total dependence on him.

—Anonymous
(Prayer, Confession)

The elegance of honesty needs no adornment.

—Merry Browne
(Truth, Speech)

Hope

Hope has two beautiful daughters. Their names are anger and courage; anger at the way things are, and courage to see that they do not remain the way they are.

—Augustine
(Anger, Courage)

Man is a creature of hope and invention, both of which belie the idea that things cannot be changed.

—Tom Clancy
(Despair, Courage)

Human Nature

God had enough for a saint and a devil, and he put it all in me.

—Johann Wolfgang Goethe
(Self-evaluation, Depravity)

So far I have never met a man who wanted to be bad. The mystery of man is that he is bad when he wants to be good.

—George MacLeod
(Depravity, Goodness)

Human nature is like a drunk peasant. Lift him into the saddle on one side, over he topples on the other side.
—Martin Luther
(Sin, Extremes)

Humility

Spiritual things are not to be boasted of. One can boast of worldly riches, and the paper money will not fly away unspent nor will the amount magically decrease, but the spiritual riches you boast of vanish with the telling.
—Watchman Nee
(Wealth, Maturity)

Until a man is nothing, God, can make nothing out of him.
—Martin Luther
(God, Discipleship)

If we are sure of our God we are free to laugh at ourselves.
—Madeleine L'Engle
(Laughter, Certainty)

Humility means two things. One, a capacity for self-criticism. . . . The second feature is allowing others to shine, affirming others, empowering and enabling others.
Those who lack humility are dogmatic and egotistical. That masks a deep sense of insecurity. They feel the success of others is at the expense of their own fame and glory.
—Cornel West
(Confidence, Affirmation)

I may have my faults, but being wrong ain't one of them.
—Jimmy Hoffa
(Self-deception, Pride)

When a little child becomes conscious of being a little child, the child-likeness is gone; and when a saint becomes conscious of being a saint, something has gone wrong.
—Oswald Chambers
(Pride, Self-awareness)

The man who knows his sins is greater than one who raises a dead man by his prayer. He who sighs and grieves within himself for an hour is greater than one who teaches the entire universe. He who follows Christ, alone and contrite, is greater than one who enjoys the favor of crowds in the churches.
—Isaac the Syrian
(Contrition, Popularity)

All men are ordinary men; the extraordinary men are those who know it.
—G.K. Chesterton
(Self-awareness, Pride)

A man is humble when he stands in the truth with a knowledge and appreciation for himself as he really is.
—*The Cloud of Unknowing*
(Self-awareness, Truth)

If you see another stumble or fall, let your first thought be that, of all men, you are most likely to stumble or fall in that same manner.
—Thomas a Kempis
(Self-awareness, Empathy)

85

Lord, when we are wrong, make us willing to change.
And when we are right, make us easy to live with.
—Peter Marshall, Sr.
(Change, Graciousness)

Humor

Anyone without a sense of humor is at the mercy of
everyone else.
—William Rotsler
(Attitude, Community)

Hypocrisy

What was so bad about [the Pharisees'] hypocrisy? . . .
They were using God and the things of God as a means
to some other end. "They do all their deeds to be noticed
by men" (Matt. 23:5). . . . Better to ignore God altogether than to exploit him as a means to something else you
value more highly.
—John Boykin
(God, Sin)

Imitation

Christian literature, to be accepted and approved by evangelical leaders of our times, must follow very closely the same train of thought, a kind of "party line" from which it is scarcely safe to depart. A half-century of this in America has made us smug and content. We imitate each other with slavish devotion. Our most strenuous efforts are put forth to try to say the same thing that everyone around us is saying—and yet to find an excuse for saying it, some little safe variation on the approved theme or, if no more, at least a new illustration.

—A.W. Tozer
(Truth, Art)

Individuals

The greatest works are done by the ones. The hundreds do not often do much—the companies never. It is the units, the single individuals, that are the power and the might.
—Charles Haddon Spurgeon
(Power, Good Works)

Influence

If you wish to enrich days, plant flowers; If you wish to enrich years, plant trees; If you wish to enrich Eternity, plant ideals in the lives of others.
—S. Truett Cathy
(Eternity, Character)

He who has influence upon the heart of God rules the world.
—Helmut Thielicke
(Prayer, God)

Insight

A new insight is quite sound when a master uses it, cheapens as it becomes popular, and is unendurable when it is merely fashionable.
—Charles Williams
(Popularity, Knowledge)

The situation today is:
Lots of knowledge, but little understanding.
Lots of means, but little meaning.
Lots of know-how, but little know-why.
Lots of sight, but little insight.
—Robert Short
(Wisdom, Knowledge)

Integrity

Integrity is keeping my commitment even if the circumstances when I made the commitment have changed.
—David Jeremiah
(Character, Perseverance)

Introspection

Look outward. You have been rightly taught Socrates' dictum that the unexamined life is not worth living. I would add: The too examined life is not worth living either.
—Charles Krauthammer
(Life, Perspective)

89

Jesus

Jesus is all we have; he is all we need and all we want.
We are shipwrecked on God and stranded on omnipotence!
—Vance Havner
(Dependence, Christ)

Follow me; I am the way, the truth, and the life.
Without the way there is no going;
Without the truth there is no knowing;
Without the life there is no living.
—Thomas a Kempis
(Christ, Truth)

To tie Jesus Christ to the very best human system is to
tie a star, light years distant, to a dead horse here on
earth. Neither the star nor Christ will thus be bound.
—Joe Bayly
(Christ, Politics)

Jesus Christ turns life right-side-up, and heaven outside-in.
—Carl F. H. Henry
(Christ, Heaven)

Joy

Surely there can be no deeper joy than that of saving souls.
—Lottie Moon
(Evangelism, Missions)

To pursue joy is to lose it. The only way to get it is to follow steadily the path of duty, without thinking of joy, and then, like sheep, it comes most surely, unsought, and we "being in the way," the angel of God, fair-haired joy, is sure to meet us.
—Alexander MacLaren
(Duty, Devotion)

Joy bursts in on our lives when we go about doing the good at hand and not trying to manipulate things and times to achieve joy.
—C. S. Lewis
(Manipulation, Ministry)

Joy is never in our power and pleasure often is.
—C. S. Lewis
(Christ, Pleasure)

This is the land of sin and death and tears . . . but up yonder is unceasing joy!
—D. L. Moody
(Heaven, Sorrow)

Judgment

I shall tell you a great secret, my friend. Do not wait for
the Last Judgment. It takes place every day.

—Albert Camus
(Eschatology, Conviction)

To sensible men, every day is a day of reckoning.

—John W. Gardner
(Reason, Accountability)

Kindness

Kindness is more important than wisdom, and the recognition of this is the beginning of wisdom.

Theodore Isaac Rubin, M.D.
(Wisdom, Love)

Kingdoms

The fundamental biblical opposition is not between flesh and Spirit, creature and Creator, but between the Creator of the flesh and its destroyer, between God and the devil, Christ and Satan, the Holy Spirit and the unholy.

—Philip S. Watson
(Spiritual Warfare, Satan)

Knowing God

You will never be satisfied just to know *about* God. Really knowing God only comes through experience as he reveals himself to you.

—Henry Blackaby
(Worship, Obedience)

Our soundest knowledge is to know that we know God not as indeed he is, neither can we know him; and our safest eloquence concerning him is our silence, when we confess, without confession, that his glory is inexplainable, his greatness above our capacity and reach.

—Richard Hooker
(Worship, Omnipotence)

Knowledge

The experts don't know for sure how old or how big the universe is. They don't know what most of it is made of. They don't know in any detail how it began or how it will end.

—*Time* magazine
(Science, Creation)

I use not only all the brains I have, but all I can borrow.

—Woodrow Wilson
(Thinking, Learning)

The beautiful, the good, the true cannot be weighed and measured. True knowledge is spiritual knowledge, which is beyond the reach of the world of quantity and therefore is disregarded by our civilization.

—Paul Tournier
(Wisdom, Virtue)

96

Labels

It seems that more than ever the compulsion today is to identify, to reduce someone to what is on the label. To identify is to control, to limit.

To love is to call by name, and so open the wide gates of creativity.
—Madeleine L'Engle
(Stereotyping, Love)

Labor

He who labors diligently need never despair; for all things are accomplished by diligence and labor.
—Menander
(Work, Despair)

Laziness

When all is said and done, as a rule, more is said than done.
—Lou Holtz
(Work, Talk)

Leadership

The job of a football coach is to make men do what they don't want to do, in order to achieve what they've always wanted to be.
—Tom Landry
(Discipleship, Teamwork)

Alexander, Caesar, and Hannibal conquered the world but they had no friends. . . . Jesus founded his empire upon love, and at this hour millions would die for him. . . . He has won the hearts of men, a task a conqueror cannot do.
—Napoleon Bonaparte
(Devotion, Motivation)

Why have we no great men? We have no great men chiefly because we are always looking for them. We are connoisseurs of greatness, and connoisseurs can never be great. . . . When anybody goes about on his hands and knees looking for a great man to worship, he is making sure that one man at any rate shall not be great.
—G. K. Chesterton
(Character, Humility)

The pioneers are the guys with the arrows in their backs.
—Erwin Potts
(Vision, Criticism)

The best decision-makers are those who are willing to suffer the most over their decisions but still retain their ability to be decisive.
—M. Scott Peck
(Compassion, Conviction)

At the end of the days of truly great leaders, the people will say about them, "We did it ourselves."

—Lao-Tzu
(Empowerment, Discipleship)

Our task is not to bring order out of chaos, but to get work done in the midst of chaos.

—George Peabody
(Productivity, Focus)

Qualifications of a pastor: He must have the mind of a scholar, the heart of a child, and the hide of a rhinoceros.

—Stuart Briscoe
(Gentleness, Courage)

There they go. I must hurry. I am their leader.

—Anonymous
(Vision, Pace-setting)

He who thinketh he leadeth and hath no one following him is only taking a walk.

—Benjamin L. Hooks
(Pace-setting, Vision)

A Christian who is ambitious to be a star disqualifies himself as a leader.

—David Watson
(Humility, Character)

One of the tests of leadership is to recognize a problem before it becomes an emergency.

—Arnold H. Glasow
(Foresight, Wisdom)

General Eisenhower used to demonstrate the art of leadership with a simple piece of string. He'd put it on a table and say: "Pull it, and it'll follow wherever you wish. Push it and it will go nowhere at all."

—Dwight D. Eisenhower
(Motivation, Discipleship)

Disturbers are to be rebuked, the low-spirited to be encouraged, the infirm to be supported, objectors confuted, the treacherous guarded against, the unskilled taught, the lazy aroused, the contentious restrained, the haughty repressed, litigants pacified, the poor relieved, the oppressed liberated, the good approved, the evil borne with, and all are to be loved. —Augustine
(Ministry, Preaching)

The trouble with being a leader today is that you can't be sure whether people are following you or chasing you. —*Bits & Pieces*
(Criticism, Courage)

It indeed seems that the Christian leader is first of all the artist who can bind together many people by his courage in giving expression to his most personal concern. —Henri Nouwen
(Honesty, Courage)

An organization can be filled by appointments, but a team must be built by a leader. —Carl Combs
(Teamwork, Discipleship)

Life

Life is the art of drawing without an eraser.
—John Christian
(Consequences, Decisions)

The monotony of life, if life is monotonous to you, is in you and not in the world.
—Phillips Brooks
(Boredom, Creation)

You must live with people to know their problems, and live with God in order to solve them.
—P. T. Forsyth
(Ministry, Discipleship)

Seek to live with such lucidity that the clarity of your motives becomes a lens which projects the image of Christ upon the screens of others' lives.
—David Augsburger
(Christlikeness, Character)

If God does not enter your kitchen, there is something wrong with your kitchen. If you can't take God into your recreation, there is something wrong with your play. . . . We all believe in the God of the heroic. What we need most these days is the God of the humdrum—the commonplace, the everyday.
—Peter Marshall
(Discipleship, God's Presence)

Listening

The most important thing in communication is to hear what isn't being said.
—Peter Drucker
(Communication, Relationships)

He who can no longer listen to his brother will soon no longer be listening to God, either.

—Dietrich Bonhoeffer
(Communication, Relationships)

Loneliness

The biggest disease today is not leprosy or cancer. It's the feeling of being uncared for, unwanted—of being deserted and alone.

—Mother Teresa
(Disease, Compassion)

Longsuffering

To become longsuffering one has to be long-bothered.

—Manford George Gutzke
(Patience, Character)

Lordship

To love and admire anything outside yourself is to take one step away from utter spiritual ruin; though we shall not be well so long as we love and admire anything more than we love and admire God.

—C. S. Lewis
(Devotion, Idolatry)

Love

When we preach atonement, it is atonement planned by love, provided by love, given by love, finished by love, necessitated because of love. When we preach the resurrection of Christ, we are preaching the miracle of love. When we preach the return of Christ, we are preaching the fulfillment of love.

—Billy Graham
(Atonement, Salvation)

God loves us the way we are, but he loves us too much
to leave us that way.   —Leighton Ford
(Change, Acceptance)

When [Jesus] wrapped a towel around his waist, poured
water into a basin, and began to wash his disciples' feet
(see John 13:4-5), Simon Peter objected that this was
beneath the dignity of the Master. We the disciples are to
be the servants, I want to insist along with Peter. But
Jesus answered him, "If I do not wash you, you have no
part in me." This is a stunning and stupendous thought.
Unless I can believe in this much love for me, unless I
can and will accept him with faith as my servant as well
as my God, unless I truly know that it's my good he
seeks, not his glory . . . then I cannot have his companionship. What an amazing revelation!
                                              —Catherine Marshall
                                              (Service, Devotion)

How do I want to be remembered? Not primarily as a
Christian scholar but rather as a loving person. This can
be the goal of every individual.   —Elton Trueblood
                                              (Legacy, Goals)

More people have been brought into the church by the
kindness of real Christian love than by all the theological arguments in the world, and more people have been
driven from the church by the hardness and ugliness of
so-called Christianity than by all the doubts in the
world.   —William Barclay
                                              (Christianity, Church)

103

The height of our love for God will never exceed the
depth of our love for one another.   —Patrick Morley
(Fellowship, Community)

Love should cast out terror, but not awe. True love must
include awe. This is one of the great truths about sex
and marriage that our age has tragically forgotten: awe
at the great mystery that is sex. . . . God is love. But love
is not *luv.* Love is not *nice.* Love is a fire, storm, earthquake, volcano, lightning, and hurricane. Love endured
the hell of the cross.
                                                      —Peter Kreeft
                                                      (Sex, Awe)

A man is only as good as what he loves.
                                                      —Saul Bellow
                                                      (Character, Devotion)

I have found the paradox that if I love until it hurts,
then there is no more hurt, but only more love.
                                                      —Mother Teresa
                                                      (Sacrifice, Suffering)

Love is never lost. If not reciprocated, it will flow back
and soften and purify the heart.   —Washington Irving
                                                      (Character, Sanctification)

If you're going to care about the fall of the sparrow you
can't pick and choose who's going to be the sparrow.
                                                      —Madeleine L'Engle
                                                      (Servanthood, Compassion)

Love is . . . a free gift. . . . And it is most itself, most free when it is offered in spite of suffering, of injustice, and of death.
—Archibald MacLeish
(Sacrifice, Servanthood)

People need love, especially when they don't deserve it.
—Unknown
(Devotion, Compassion)

The Bible tells us to love our neighbors, and also to love our enemies; probably because they are generally the same people.
—G. K. Chesterton
(Neighbors, Enemies)

Christians state glibly that they love the whole world, while they permit themselves animosities within their immediate world. . . . But loving the world at large can only be done by loving face to face the world that is not so distant.
—Calvin Miller
(Compassion, World)

Lying

A lie is like a snowball. The longer it is rolled on the ground the larger it becomes.
—Martin Luther
(Consequences, Sin)

M

Marriage

The difficulty with marriage is that we fall in love with a personality but must live with a character.

—Peter DeVries
(Family, Love)

In domestic affairs, I am led by Katie [my wife]. In all other matters, I am led by the Holy Ghost.

—Martin Luther
(Holy Spirit, Submission)

Marriage is somewhat like undertaking a Lego project without instructions.

—Ammunni Bala Subramanian
(Husbands, Wives)

The concept of two people living together for 25 years without a serious dispute suggests a lack of spirit only to be admired in sheep.

—Walter Lippman
(Conflict, Timidity)

Martyrdom

The blood of the martyrs is the seed of the church.

—Tertullian
(Sacrifice, Church)

Materialism

The late Bishop Edwin Hughes once delivered a rousing sermon on "God's Ownership" that offended a rich parishioner. The wealthy man took the bishop off for lunch, and then walked him through his elaborate gardens, woodlands, and farm. "Now are you going to tell me," he demanded when the tour was completed, that all this land does not belong to me?" Bishop Hughes smiled and suggested, "Ask me that same question a hundred years from now."

(Eternity, Greed)

The essence of life today is not having—it is having to have.

—David Hansen
(Greed, Lifestyle)

The world would be better off if people tried to become better. And people would become better if they stopped trying to become better off. For when everybody tries to become better off, nobody becomes better off. But when everybody tries to become better, everybody is better off.

—Peter Maurin
(Service, Greed)

Media

I keep reading between the lies.

—Goodman Ace
(Deception, Culture)

Meditation

A garment that is double dyed, dipped again and again, will retain the color a great while; so a truth which is the subject of meditation.
—Philip Henry
(Truth, Study)

Meekness

The meek man is not a human mouse afflicted with a sense of his own inferiority. Rather, he may be in his moral life as bold as a lion and as strong as Samson; but he has stopped being fooled about himself. He has accepted God's estimate of his own life. He knows he is as weak and helpless as God has declared him to be, but paradoxically, he knows at the same time that he is, in the sight of God, more important than angels.

—A. W. Tozer
(Courage, Self-evaluation)

Memories

You can close your eyes to reality but not to memories.
—Stanislaw J. Lee
(Deception, Denial)

Men

There is one unmistakable lesson in American history: a community that allows a large number of young men to grow up in broken families, dominated by women, never acquiring any stable relationship to male authority, never acquiring any set of rational expectations about the future—that community asks for and gets chaos. Crime, violence, unrest, disorder—most particularly the furious, unrestrained lashing out at the whole social structure—that is not only to be expected; it is very near to inevitable.

—Daniel Patrick Moynihan
(Family, Society)

Mercy

We are God's tenants here, and yet here he, our landlord, pays us rents—not yearly, nor quarterly, but hourly and quarterly; every minute he renews his mercy.

—John Donne
(Grace, Hope)

Ministry

If you are a Christian, then you are a minister. A non-ministering Christian is a contradiction in terms.

—D. Elton Trueblood
(Lifestyle, Example)

The three qualifications for the ministry are the grace of God, knowledge of the sacred Scriptures, and gumption.

—Samuel Johnson
(Scripture, Character)

Our office is a ministry of grace and salvation. It subjects us to great burdens and labors, dangers and temptations, with little reward or gratitude from the world. But Christ himself will be our reward if we labor faithfully.
—Martin Luther
(Sacrifice, Servanthood)

It is one of the ironies of the ministry that the very man who works in God's name is often hardest put to find time for God. The parents of Jesus lost him at church, and they were not the last ones to lose him there.
—Vance Havner
(Time, Priorities)

A pastor needs three bones to remain upright: a backbone, a wish bone, and a funny bone.
—Anonymous
(Courage, Hope)

Shun, as you would the plague, a cleric who from being poor has become wealthy, or who from being nobody has become a celebrity.
—Jerome
(Fame, Pride)

Ministers are like trumpets, which make no sound if breath be not breathed into them. Or like Ezekiel's wheels, which move not unless the Spirit move them. Or like Elisha's servants whose presence does no good unless Elisha's spirit be there also.
—John Flavel
(Holy Spirit, Unction)

When a minister is "too charming," he is always in demand for events of small spiritual significance.
—Paul M. Schmidt
(Character, Leadership)

Ministers cannot walk on water; but they can learn to swim.
—Edward Bratcher
(Leadership, Discipleship)

God makes his ministers a flame of fire. Am I ignitable? God, deliver me from the dread asbestos of "other things." Saturate me with the oil of thy Spirit that I may be a flame. Make me thy fuel, Flame of God.
—Jim Elliot
(Holy Spirit, Unction)

Misfortune

Mishaps are like knives, that either serve us or cut us, as we grasp them by the blade or the handle.
—James Russell Lowell
(Perspective, Pain)

Missions

We are all missionaries. Wherever we go, we either bring people nearer to Christ, or we repel them from Christ.
—Eric Liddell
(Evangelism, Example)

We have a whole Christ for our salvation, a whole Bible for our staff, a whole church for our fellowship, and a whole world for our parish.
—John Chrysostom
(Evangelism, Salvation)

The mission of the church is missions.
—Unknown
(Church, Goals)

Mistakes

Strong people make as many and as ghastly mistakes as weak people. The difference is that strong people admit them, laugh at them, learn from them. That is how they become strong.
—Richard J. Needham
(Failure, Maturity)

Money

For every verse in the Bible that tells us the benefits of wealth, there are ten that tell us the danger of wealth.
—Haddon Robinson
(Materialism, Greed)

Money will buy a bed but not sleep; books but not brains; food but not appetite; finery but not beauty; a house but not a home; medicine but not health; luxuries but not culture; amusements but not happiness; religion but not salvation—a passport to everywhere but heaven.
—*Voice in the Wilderness*
(Materialism, Satisfaction)

God entrusts us with money as a test; for like a toy to the child, it is training for handling things of more value.
—Fred Smith
(Testing, Character)

Satan now is wiser than of yore. And tempts by making rich, not by making poor.
—Alexander Pope
(Materialism, Wealth)

When a fellow says, "It isn't the money but the principle of the thing"—it's the money.
—Kin Hubbard
(Integrity, Lying)

Jesus talked much about money. Sixteen of the thirty-eight parables were concerned with how to handle money and possessions. In the Gospels, an amazing one out of ten verses deal directly with the subject of money. The Bible offers 500 verses on prayer, less than 500 verses on faith, but more than 2,000 verses on money and possessions.
—Howard L. Dayton, Jr.
(Bible, Materialism)

There is no dignity quite so impressive, and no independence quite so important, as living within your means.
—Calvin Coolidge
(Stewardship, Giving)

114

He that serves God for money will serve the Devil for better wages.
—Sir Robert L'Estrange
(Devil, Service)

Get all you can.
Save all you can.
Give all you can.
—John Wesley
(Saving, Giving)

Nothing that is God's is obtainable by money.
—Tertullian
(Wealth, Salvation)

Almost all reformers, however strict their social conscience, live in houses as big as they can pay for.
—Logan Pearsall Smith
(Consience, Materialism)

Mothers

Let France have good mothers and she will have good sons.
—Napoleon
(Sons, Parenting)

All I am my mother made me.
—John Quincy Adams
(Parenting, Character)

I believe in the love of all mothers,
and its importance in the lives of the children they bear.
It is stronger than steel, softer than down,
and more resilient than a green sapling on the hillside.
It closes wounds, melts disappointments,
and enables the weakest child to stand tall
and straight in the fields of adversity.
I believe that this love, even at its best,
is only a shadow of the love of God . . .
And I believe that one of the most beautiful sights
in the world is a mother who lets this greater love
flow through her to her child,
blessing the world with the tenderness of her touch
and the tears of her joy.

—John Killinger
(Love, Sacrifice)

Motivation

The oil can is mightier than the sword.

—Everett Dirksen
(Complaining, Leadership)

Motives

No man knows what he is living for until he knows
what he'll die for.

—Peter Pertocci
(Causes, Courage)

God uses lust to impel man to marriage, ambition to
office, avarice to earning, and fear to faith.

—Martin Luther
(Sin, Character)

Music

The Devil should not be allowed to keep all the best
tunes for himself.
—Martin Luther
(Devil, Worship)

Next after theology, I give to music the highest place and
the greatest honor.
—Martin Luther
(Theology, Worship)

Narcissism

You cannot at the same time show that Christ is wonderful—and you are clever.   —Principal Denny of Scotland
(Witness, Christ)

Christ sends none away empty but those who are full of
themselves.   —Donald Gray Barnhouse
(Emptiness, Gifts)

I talk to myself because I like dealing with a better class
of people.   —Jackie Mason
(Arrogance, Self-absorption)

Nature

Nature is the art of God.

—Thomas Brown
(Creation, Art)

Neglect

The untended garden will soon be overrun with weeds; the heart that fails to cultivate truth and root out error will shortly be a theological wilderness.　　—A. W. Tozer
(Error, Truth)

Neighbors

The Bible tells us to love our neighbors, and also to love our enemies; probably because generally they are the same people.　　—G. K. Chesterton
(Love, Enemies)

New Age

I don't . . . think any real journey is beginning with the New Age movement. I think it's more a detour, a truck stop on the way to the Rockies.　　—Peggy Noonan
(Religion, Mysticism)

120

Obedience

If God be God over us, we must yield him universal obedience in all things. He must not be over us in one thing, and under us in another, but he must be over us in everything.
—Peter Bulkeley
(Sovereignty, Submission)

The fruit of the Spirit grows only in the garden of obedience.
—Terry Fullam
(Lifestyle, Character)

Do not quench the Spirit. . . . When it moves and stirs in you, be obedient; but do not go beyond, nor add to it, nor take from it.
—George Fox
(Holy Spirit, Devotion)

All the good maxims have been written. It only remains to put them into practice.
—Blaise Pascal
(Lifestyle, Action)

It is our business to see that we do right; God will see
that we come out right.   —Donald Gray Barnhouse
(Discipleship, Character)

He that cannot obey, cannot command.
—Benjamin Franklin
(Leadership, Character)

Opportunity
When one door closes, another opens; but we often look
so long and so regretfully upon the closed door that we
do not see the one which has opened for us.
—Alexander Graham Bell
(Future, Regret)

Opposition
We are so outnumbered there's only one thing to do. We
must attack.   —Sir Andrew Cunningham
(Courage, Trials)

P

Parables

You cannot tell people what to do, you can only tell
them parables; and that is what art really is, particular
stories of particular people and experiences.

—W. H. Auden
(Preaching, Communication)

Parenting

The parent who exerts his or her power most drastically
over children loses all power over them, except the
power to twist and hurt and destroy. —Garry Wills
(Power, Children)

My major effort must be devoted to my children. If
Caroline and John turn out badly, nothing I could do in
the public eye would have any meaning.

—Jacqueline Kennedy Onassis
Shortly after she entered the White House in 1960
(Children, Fame)

Passion

The core problem is not that we are too passionate about bad things, but that we are not passionate enough about good things.
—Larry Crabb
(Conviction, Goodness)

Patience

Second only to suffering, waiting may be the greatest teacher and trainer in godliness, maturity, and genuine spirituality most of us ever encounter.
—Richard Hendrix
(Maturity, Godliness)

God's Word often refers to the Christian experience as a walk, seldom as a run, and never as a mad dash.
—Steven J. Cole
(Stress, Burnout)

He is not truly patient who will suffer only as much as he pleases or from whom he pleases. A truly patient man gives no heed from whom he suffers, whether from his superior or from his equal or from someone below him.
—Thomas a Kempis
(Suffering, Surrender)

Peace

Have peace in your heart, and thousands will be saved around you.
—Seraphin of Sarov
(Salvation, Witness)

Peace is not the absence of trouble. Peace is the presence of God.
—Unknown
(God's Presence, Difficulty)

God . . . "works always in tranquility." Fuss and feverishness, anxiety, intensity, intolerance, instability, pessimism and wobble, and every kind of hurry and worry—these, even on the highest levels, are signs of the self-made and self-acting soul; the spiritual parvenu. The saints are never like that. They share the quiet and noble qualities of the great family to which they belong.
—Evelyn Underhill
(Self-reliance, Stress)

Persecution

The greatest criticism of the church today is that no one wants to persecute it: because there is nothing very much to persecute it about.
—George F. MacLeod
(Church, Conviction)

Perseverance

To cling to God and to the things of God—this must be our major effort, this must be the road that the heart follows.
—John Cassian
(God, Heart)

Never, never, never, never give up.
—Winston Churchill
(Quitting, Endurance)

125

The woman who stayed behind to seek Christ was the only one to see him. Fpr perseverance is esstial to any good deed, as the voice of truth tells us: "Whosoever perseveres to the end will be saved."   —Gregory the Great
(Good Works, Christ)

Let me tell you the secret that has led me to my goal. My strength lies solely in my tenacity.   —Louis Pasteur
(Tenacity, Success)

Perspective

My grandmother used to tell me that every boss is temporary, that every rainy day is temporary, that every hardship is temporary. She used to tell me, "Son, every goodbye ain't gone. Just hold on—there's joy coming in the morning."   —James Melvin Washington
(Difficulty, Hope)

If the only tool you have is a hammer, you tend to see every problem as a nail.   —Abraham Maslow
(Leadership, Solutions)

You are given a situation. What you are determines what you see; what you see determines what you do.
    —Haddon Robinson
(Solutions, Leadership)

The young man who has not wept is a savage, and the old man who will not laugh is a fool.
    —George Santayana
(Grief, Laughter)

The greatest thing a human soul ever does in this world

is to see something and tell what it saw in a plain way. Hundreds of people can talk for one who can think, but thousands can think for one who can see. To see clearly is poetry, prophecy, and religion, all in one.

—John Ruskin
(Leadership, Vision)

Politics

Too many of us Christians confuse political convictions with spiritual convictions. Insecure with ambiguity, we assume people of one Lord, one faith, and one baptism must also promote one political agenda. That assumption leads the church into trouble. First, it prompts us to make judgments about people that ought to be left to God. . . . Second, when the church confuses spiritual and political convictions it is tempted to use political power to forward a "spiritual" agenda.   —Don Ratzlaff
(Judgment, Conviction)

What's real in politics is what the voters decide is real.

Ben J. Wattenberg
(Truth, Values)

Popularity

To set one's heart on being popular is fatal to the preacher's best growth. It is the worst and feeblest part of your congregation that makes itself heard in vociferous applause, and it applauds that in you which pleases it.

—Phillips Brooks
(Pride, Deception)

Possessions

The more you have the less you can give, and the less
you have the more you can give.　　　—Mother Teresa
(Giving, Materialism)

Poverty

The spiritual poverty of the Western world is much
greater than the physical poverty of our people. You in
the West have millions of people who suffer such
terrible loneliness and emptiness.　　　—Mother Teresa
(Loneliness, Meaninglessness)

Power

Do not pray for easy lives; pray to be stronger people.
Do not pray for tasks equal to your powers; pray for
powers equal to your tasks. Then the doing of your
work shall be no miracle, but you shall be a miracle.
Every day you shall wonder at the richness of life which
has come to you by the grace of God.

—Phillips Brooks
(Responsibility, Laziness)

Praise

When we admonish people to praise, don't tell them
what they'll get out of it, or what God will get out of it.
Tell them to praise him simply because it is right and
reasonable to do so. To attach anything more to this is to
presume undue importance upon ourselves.

—John Fischer
(Worship, Music)

God hates those who praise themselves.

—Clement
(Pride, Boasting)

Prayer

Every time we pray, our horizon is altered, our attitude
to things is altered, not sometimes but every time, and
the amazing thing is that we don't pray more.

—Oswald Chambers
(Attitude, Character)

It would be rash to say that there is any prayer in which
God never grants. But the strongest candidate is the
prayer we might express in the single word encore.

—C. S. Lewis
(Presumption, Answers)

When life knocks you to your knees—well, that's the
best position in which to pray, isn't it?   —Ethel Barrymore
(Humility, Submission)

Satan trembles when he sees
The weakest saint upon his knees.

—Hymnwriters William Cowper and John Newton
(Humility, Power)

The goal, the highest good, of the human creature is
that the knowledge of God and prayer to God converge.

—Eugene Peterson
(Knowing God, Submission)

Any revitalization of faith in this country will have to
start with prayer, in which we gain a sense of the living
presence of God.   —George H. Gallup, Jr.
(Repentance, Renewal)

We honor God when we ask for great things. It is a humiliating thing to think that we are satisfied with very small results.
—D. L. Moody
(Honor, Satisfaction)

Heaven is full of answers to prayers for which no one ever bothered to ask.
—Billy Graham
(Heaven, Apathy)

I am often, I believe, praying for others when I should be doing things for them. It's so much easier to pray for a bore than to go and see him.
—C. S. Lewis
(Action, Good Works)

Souls without prayer are like people whose bodies or limbs are paralyzed: they possess feet and hands but they cannot control them.
—Teresa of Avila
(Growth, Self-control)

In prayer it is better to have a heart without words than words without heart.
—John Bunyan
(Sincerity, Conviction)

I have often learned more in one prayer than I have been able to glean from much reading and reflection.
—Martin Luther
(Study, Learning)

He who prays fervently knows not whether he prays or not, for he is not thinking of the prayer which he makes, but of God, to whom he makes it.
—Francis de Sales
(Devotion, Submission)

As we are involved in unceasing thinking, so we are called to unceasing prayer.   —Henri Nouwen
(Spirituality, Devotion)

I have been driven many times to my knees by the over-whelming conviction that I had nowhere else to go. My wisdom, and that of all about me, seemed insufficient for the day.   —Abraham Lincoln
(Seeking God, Submission)

In prayer, we are aware that God is in action and that when the circumstances are ready, when others are in the right place, and when our hearts are prepared, he will call us into the action. Waiting in prayer is a disciplined refusal to act before God acts.   —Eugene Peterson
(Waiting, Trust)

Not to want to pray is the sin behind sin.
—P. T. Forsyth
(Prayerlessness, Sin)

To pray is the greatest thing we can do, and to do it well, there must be calmness, time, and deliberation.
—E. M. Bounds
(Time, Devotion)

The penalty of not praying is the loss of one's capacity to pray.   —Edward J. Farrell
(Spiritual Neglect, Apathy)

Pray the largest prayers. You cannot think a prayer so large that God, in answering it, will not wish you had made it larger. Pray not for crutches but for wings!

—Phillips Brooks
(Faith, Hope)

We are too busy to pray, and so we are too busy to have power. We have a great deal of activity but we accomplish little; many services but few conversions; much machinery but few results.

—R. A. Torrey
(Power, Results)

Preaching

O God, let me preach with enthusiasm because of what Christ did, not because of what the crowds think . . . because of the salvation we have, not the size of the group we have. Use me, O God, not because it's the hour for the message, but because you've given me a message for the hour.

—Ed Towne
(Conviction, Obedience)

No man is fit to preach the gospel, seeing the whole world is set against it, save only he who is armed to suffer.

—John Calvin
(Suffering, Opposition)

If you ask me how you may shorten your sermons, I should say, study them better. Spend more time in the study that you may need less in the pulpit. We are generally longest when we have least to say.

—Charles Spurgeon
(Study, Speech)

Those who make comfort the great subject of their preaching seem to mistake the end of their ministry. Holiness is the great end. There must be a struggle and trial here. Comfort is a cordial, but no one drinks cordials from morning to night.   —John Henry Newman
(Holiness, Prophetic Voice)

To be always relevant, you have to say things which are eternal.   —Simone Weil
(Eternity, Relevance)

It is not necessary for a preacher to express all his thoughts in one sermon. A preacher should have three principles, first, to make a good beginning and not spend time with many words before coming to the point; secondly, to say that which belongs to the subject in chief, and avoid strange and foreign thought; thirdly, to stop at the proper time.   —Martin Luther
(Brevity, Speech)

I've heard a lot of sermons in the past ten years or so that made me want to get up and walk out. They're secular, psychological, self-help sermons. Friendly, but of no use. They didn't make you straighten up. They didn't give you anything hard. . . . At some point and in some way, a sermon has to direct people toward the death of Christ and the campaign that God has waged over the centuries to get our attention.   —Garrison Keillor
(Conviction, Cross)

133

To preach more than half an hour, a man should be an angel himself or have angels for hearers.

—George Whitefield
(Brevity, Longsuffering)

When pride has written the sermon, it goes with us to the pulpit.

—Richard Baxter
(Pride, Motives)

To love to preach is one thing—to love those to whom we preach, quite another.

—Richard Cecil
(Compassion, Motives)

Surely the preacher's greatest sin is to put people to sleep with the greatest story ever told.

—Bruce W. Thielemann
(Boredom, Gospel)

Preaching is not the art of making a sermon and delivering it. Preaching is the art of making a preacher and delivering him.

—Bishop Quayle
(Sanctification, Holiness)

All preachers must struggle for that magical note somewhere between a trumpet of uncertain sound that brings no one to battle and the tin horn that thinks itself to be Gabriel's.

—Robert N. Schaper
(Conviction, Pride)

The test of a preacher is that his congregation goes away saying, not "What a lovely sermon!" but "I will do something."

—Francis de Sales
(Action, Persuasion)

The true function of a preacher is to disturb the comfortable and to comfort the disturbed.　　　—Chad Walsh
(Complacency, Comfort)

Preparation
A lasting work requires extensive preparation.
　　　—Douglas Rumford
(Endurance, Work)

Pressure
When three are shut into a furnace and three become four, that is enlargement through pressure.
　　　—Watchman Nee
(Difficulty, God's Presence)

The intensity of pressure doesn't matter as much as its location. Does it come between you and God, or does it press you closer to him?　　　—Unknown
(Devotion, Rebellion)

Pride
A man is never so proud as when striking an attitude of humility!　　　—C. S. Lewis
(Humility, Self-deception)

I define ego as Edging God Out.

　　　—Kenneth Blanchard
(God, Self-reliance)

It's like the beaver told the rabbit as they stared up at the immense wall of Hoover Dam, "No, I didn't actually build it myself. But it was based on an idea of mine."

—Charles H. Townes
Nobel Prize winner in laser technology
(Humility, Ambition)

Priorities

We must first be committed to Christ, then to one another in Christ, and finally to the work of Christ in the world.

—Ray Ortlund
(Goals, Commitment)

Whenever we place a higher priority on solving our problems than on pursuing God, we are immoral.

—Larry Crabb
(Problem-Solving, Immorality)

Think of only three things—your God, your family, and the Green Bay Packers—in that order. —Vince Lombardi
(God, Family)

Problems

There are three kinds of people in our society: those who can't see or refuse to see the problems; those who see the problems and because they didn't personally create them are content to blame someone else; and those who see the problems and though they didn't create them are willing to assume personal responsibility for solving them.

—John Perkins
(Servanthood, Ministry)

Prosperity

Prosperity has not been kind to the American family. It breeds short, shallow roots. Fragile anchors. It's not that prosperity and wealth are inherently evil. They aren't. But their presence constantly tempts us to believe we are secure without God and that money can be an adequate substitute for real family values. —Robert Lewis
(Security, Materialism)

Protection

God has promised to keep his people, and he will keep his promise. —Charles Haddon Spurgeon
(Promises, God)

Provision

God's work done in God's way will never lack God's supply. —J. Hudson Taylor
(God, Ministry)

Purity

The pastor should always be pure in thought, inasmuch as no impurity ought to pollute him who has undertaken the office of wiping away the stains of pollution in the hearts of others . . . for the hand that would cleanse from dirt must be clean, lest, being itself sordid with clinging mire, it soil whatever it touches all the more. —Gregory the Great
(Ministry, Example)

Purpose

Great minds have purposes; others have wishes.
—Washington Irving
(Vision, Wishful Thinking)

Two centuries ago, when a great man appeared, people looked for God's purpose in him. Today we look for his press agent.
—Daniel Boorstin
(Fame, Popularity)

Questions

God will answer all our questions in one way and one way only—namely, by showing us more of his Son.

—Watchman Nee
(Jesus, Revelation)

When somebody says, "That's a good question," you can be pretty sure it's a lot better than the answer you're going to get.

—Franklin P. Jones
(Certainty, Truth)

It is harder to ask a sensible question than to supply a sensible answer.

—Persian proverb
(Wisdom, Knowledge)

Quitting

It is always too soon to quit.

—V. Raymond Edman
(Faithfulness, Integrity)

Quitting

Quitting is usually a long-term solution to a short-term problem.

—Anonymous
(Conflict, Faithfulness)

Reconciliation

One sign and wonder . . . that alone can prove the
power of the gospel is that of reconciliation . . . Hindus
can produce as many miracles as any Christian miracle
worker. Islamic saints in India can produce and duplicate every miracle that has been produced by Christians.
But they cannot duplicate the miracle of black and white
together, of racial injustice being swept away by the
power of the gospel. —Vinay Samuel
(Miracles, Racial Injustice)

Religion

It is a great mistake to think that God is chiefly interested in religion. —William Temple
(God, Faith)

If your religion does not change you, then you should
change your religion. —Elbert Hubbard
(Change, Faith)

Religion is, at its heart, a way of denying the authority
of the rest of the world.　　　　　　　　—Stephen Carter
(Culture, Authority)

Religion is the best armor a man can have, but it is the
worst cloak.　　　　　　　　　　　　　—John Bunyan
(Hypocrisy, Strength)

Men will wrangle for religion; write for it; fight for it;
die for it; anything but live for it.　　　　—C. C. Colton
(Lifestyle, Faith)

It is no disgrace to Christianity, it is no disgrace to any
great religion, that its counsels of perfection have not
made every single person perfect. If, after centuries, a
disparity is still found between its ideal and its followers, it only means that the religion still maintains the
ideal, and the followers still need it.　　—G. K. Chesterton
(Christianity, Perfection)

History shows that when religion wanes in any country,
it is not replaced by popular rationalist philosophy that
leads to a universal happiness and peace . . . The vacu-
um left by the waning of religion in western countries
has been filled by an army of superstitious cults and
beliefs. Perfect secularism by no means casts out fear.
　　　　　　　　　　　　　　　　　—David H. C. Read
(Superstition, Secularism)

Religious Freedom

I have learned that the important thing for the church is not to have leaders and parish buildings, but to have Christians in the individual parishes who take the Gospel and the sacraments seriously. . . . This was a lesson for us. We had always had the church as an institution. The pastor would go to the mayor and ask for money to fix the roof. The pastor got his money and had a lifelong job; he could lose it only for reasons of immorality. . . . In the Confessing Church, we learned to give all this up—and to learn this in only twelve years is a great gift.
—Pastor Friedemann M.
Remembering his years under Hitler
(Separation, Sacrifice)

Renewal

We're in need of a spiritual revival.
—Television producer Norman Lear
(Revival, Awakening)

Repentance

A salty pagan, full of the juices of life, is a hundred times dearer to God, and also far more attractive to men, than a scribe who knows his Bible . . . in whom none of this results in repentance, action, and above all, death of the self. A terrible curse hangs over the know-it-all who does nothing.
—Helmut Thielicke
(Hypocrisy, Apathy)

Reputation

Be more concerned with your character than with your reputation, because your character is what you really are, while your reputation is merely what others think you are.

—John Wooden
(Character, Lifestyle)

Rest

I used to say that the Devil never takes a vacation, so why should I?—and I never stopped to think that the Devil wasn't to be my example.

—Anonymous
(Devil, Vacation)

When I rest, I rust.

—Martin Luther
(Lethargy, Work)

Resurrection

Jesus' resurrection makes it impossible for man's story to end in chaos—it has to move inexorably towards light, towards life, towards love.

—Carolo Carretto
(Hope, Eternal Life)

Revelation

I lay it down as a foundation principle . . . that [God's] voice will always be in harmony with itself, no matter in how many different ways he may speak. The voices may be many, the message can be but one. If God tells me in one voice to do or to leave undone anything, he cannot possibly tell me the opposite in another voice. . . . Therefore my rule for distinguishing the voice of God would be to bring it to the test of this harmony.
—Hannah Whitall Smith
(Guidance, God's Will)

Risk

He who deliberates fully before taking a step will spend his entire life on one leg. —Chinese proverb
(Cowardice, Timidity)

Strangely, the expounders of many of the great new ideas of history were frequently considered on the lunatic fringe for some or all of their lives. If one stands up and is counted, from time to time one may get knocked down. But remember this: a man flattened by an opponent can get up again. A man flattened by conformity stays down for good. —Thomas J. Watson, Jr.
(Failure, Peer Pressure)

Take calculated risks. That is quite different from being rash. —George S. Patton
(Rashness, Reason)

Shoot for the moon. Even if you miss it, you will land among the stars.
—Les Brown
(Achievement, Results)

Rumor

Rumor travels faster, but it don't stay put as long as truth.
—Will Rogers
(Truth, Gossip)

Sabbath

All days are holy, but some are more so; all moments can be sacred, but not unless we set some aside to be intensely so.
—Karen Mains
(Holiness, Time)

I can't be teaching kids how to keep the Lord's Day holy while my cash registers are ringing.
—S. Truett Cathy
Chick-Fil-A restaurant chain owner and
Sunday school teacher, whose stores close on Sundays
(Example, Work)

He who wants to enter the holiness of the day must first lay down the profanity of clattering commerce, of being yoked to toil. He must go away from the screech of dissonant days, from the nervousness and fury of acquisitiveness and the betrayal in embezzling his own life. He must say farewell to manual work and learn to understand that the world has already been created.
—Abraham Joshua Heschel
(Profanity, Holiness)

Sacrifice

A life without sacrifices is abomination.

—Annie Dillard
(Discipleship, Lifestyle)

We all have some dying to do. Jesus showed us how it should be done.

—Stephen Neill
(Servanthood, Death)

The pendulum is swinging back from self-expression to self-discipline. But if we are serious about this, it means we will have to sacrifice some measure of the freedom we now have to do anything we want if it feels good.

—Michael Horowitz
(Indulgence, Self-discipline)

The willing sacrifice of the innocent is the most powerful answer yet conceived by God or man to insolent tyranny.

—Mohandas Gandhi
(Tyranny, Social Justice)

Salvation

If we or the world could be saved through human kindness or clear thinking, Jesus either would have formed a sensitivity group and urged us to share our feelings or would have founded a school and asked us to have discussions. But knowing the ways of God, the way of the world, and the persistence of human sin, he took up the cross, called disciples, gathered the church, and bade us follow him down a different path of freedom.

—William H. Willimon
(Sin, Cross)

Salvation isn't what liberals or conservatives in this country think it is. It's about getting my life straight. It's not about ultimate significance. Salvation is about an adventure that was made possible through the death and resurrection of Jesus of Nazareth, through which I am made part of a community who will tell me who I am. You are not free to make up your life as a Christian. Your life is not like a gift, your life is a gift. That is a very important grammatical point. Until you learn to receive your life gift, you are lost. And people are lost.
—Stanley Hauerwas
(Life, Gifts)

You can become a Christian by going to church just about as easily as you can become an automobile by sleeping in a garage.
—Vance Havner
(Lifestyle, Church)

Sanctification

O Lord, make the bad people good and the good people nice.
—Prayer of a young girl
(Hypocrisy, Meanness)

A saint is someone whose life makes it easier to believe in God.
—William Barclay
(Witness, Example)

God creates out of nothing. Wonderful, you say. Yes, to be sure, but he does what is still more wonderful: He makes saints out of sinners.
—Soren Kierkegaard
(Sin, Creation)

A walloping great congregation is fine, and fun, but
what most communities really need is a couple of saints.
—Martin Thornton
(Church, Holiness)

Satan
We may not pay [Satan] reverence, for that would be
indiscreet, but we can at least respect his talents. A person who has for untold centuries maintained the impos-
ing position of spiritual head of four-fifths of the human
race, and political head of the whole of it, must be
granted the possession of executive abilities of the lofti-
est order.
—Mark Twain
(Sin, Evil)

Satisfaction
I have never met a soul who has set out to satisfy the
Lord and has not been satisfied himself.
—Watchman Nee
(Contentment, Lordship)

Science
We have grasped the mystery of the atom and rejected
the Sermon on the Mount.
—Omar Bradley
(Atomic Age, Ethics)

Scripture
My conscience has been taken captive by the Word of
God, and to go against conscience or Scripture is neither
right nor safe.
—Martin Luther
(Conscience, Obedience)

To hear the voice of God in Holy Scripture oneself, and to help others to hear it, is a worthy cause to which to devote one's resources. To be commissioned to this cause is a sacred trust, not to be undertaken lightly, not to be refused irresponsibly, but to be fulfilled thankfully.
—F. F. Bruce
(God's Voice, Calling)

Most people are bothered by those Scriptures passages which they cannot understand. But for me, the passages in Scripture which trouble me most are those which I do understand.
—Mark Twain
(Understanding, Obedience)

Ignorance of the Scriptures is ignorance of Christ.
—Jerome
(Christ, Ignorance)

If someone considers the prophetic writings with all the diligence and reverence they are worth, while he reads and examines with great care, it is certain that in that very act he will be struck in his mind and senses by some more divine breath and will recognize that the books he reads have not been produced in a human way, but are words of God.
—Origen
(Revelation, Conviction)

Second Coming
I wish I could be alive when Christ returns because I would like to be the first earthly monarch to take my crown and lay it at his feet.
—Elizabeth I of England
(Worship, Majesty)

Self-control

Be not angry that you cannot make others as you wish them to be, since you cannot make yourself as you wish to be.
—Thomas a Kempis
(Change, Acceptance)

O God, help us to be masters of ourselves that we may be servants of others.
—Sir Alec Paterson
(Discipline, Ministry)

Self-deception

Knowing your own strength is a fine thing. Recognizing your own weakness is even better. What is really bad, what hurts and finally defeats us, is mistaking a weakness for a strength.
—Sydney J. Harris
(Discernment, Strength)

You never find yourself until you face the truth.
—Pearl Bailey
(Truth, Discernment)

Self-examination

It is when we face ourselves and face Christ, that we are lost in wonder, love and praise. We need to rediscover the almost lost discipline of self-examination; and then a re-awakened sense of sin will beget a re-awakened sense of wonder.
—Andrew Murray
(Wonder, Sin)

Self-fulfillment

The search for self-fulfillment is endless, and endlessly frustrating.

—James Hitchcock
(Frustration, Service)

Living for his own pleasure is the least pleasurable thing a man can do; if his neighbors don't kill him in disgust, he will die slowly of boredom and lovelessness.

—Joy Davidman
(Selfishness, Pride)

Self-love

The labor of self-love is a heavy one indeed. Think for yourself whether much of your sorrow has not arisen from someone speaking slightly of you. As long as you set yourself up as a little god to which you must be loyal, there will be those who will delight to offer affront to your idol. How then can you hope to have inward peace? The heart's fierce effort to protect itself from every slight, to shield its touchy honor from the bad opinion of friend and enemy, will never let the mind rest.

—A. W. Tozer
(Pride, Idolatry)

The reigning cliche of the day is that in order to love others one must first learn to love oneself. This formulation—love thyself, then thy neighbor—is a license for unremitting self-indulgence, because the quest for self-love is endless. By the time you have finally learned to love yourself, you'll find yourself playing golf at Leisure World.

—Charles Krauthammer
(Self-indulgence, Love)

The smallest package I ever saw was a man wrapped up wholly in himself.
—Billy Graham
(Selfishness, Arrogance)

Self-reliance

You cannot help men permanently by doing for them what they could and should do themselves.
—Abraham Lincoln
(Independence, Ministry)

O what a giant is man when he fights against himself, and what a dwarf when he needs or exercises his own assistance for himself. . . . Man hath no center but misery; there, and only there, he is fixed, and sure to find himself.
—John Donne
(Misery, Human Nature)

Service

Teach us, Lord, to serve you as you deserve, to give and not to count the cost, to fight and not to heed the wounds, to toil and not to seek for rest, to labor and not to ask for any reward save that of knowing that we do your will.
—Ignatius Loyola
(Discipleship, Sacrifice)

Beware of anything that competes with loyalty to Jesus Christ. The greatest competitor of devotion to Jesus is service for him.
—Oswald Chambers
(Loyalty, Christ)

Sex

You mustn't force sex to do the work of love, or love to
do the work of sex.
—Mary McCarthy
(Love, Marriage)

Sickness

God is often (in some senses) nearer to us, and
more effectually present with us, in sickness than in
health. . . . He often sends diseases of the body to cure
those of the soul. Comfort yourself with the sovereign
Physician of both the soul and the body.
—Brother Lawrence
(Healing, Soul)

Silence

To preserve the silence within—amid all the noise. To
remain open and quiet, a moist humus in the fertile
darkness where the rain falls and the grain ripens—no
matter how many tramp across the parade ground in
whirling dust under an arid sky.
—Dag Hammarskjold
(Contemplation, Prayer)

To sin by silence when they should protest makes cow-
ards out of men.
—Abraham Lincoln
(Protest, Cowardice)

Speech is silver; silence is gold.
— Proverb
(Speech, Values)

155

Sin

Many Christians define sin as the sum total of acts which they themselves do not commit.

—Carlyle Marney
(Self-evaluation, Pride)

I have more trouble with D. L. Moody than any other man I know.

—D. L. Moody
(Self-awareness, Character)

You can't repent of confusion of psychological flaws inflicted by your parents—you're stuck with them. But you can repent of sin. Sin and repentance are the only grounds for hope and joy. The grounds for reconciled, joyful relationships. You can be born again.

—John Alexander
(Repentance, Confession)

Contrary to popular opinion, sin is not what you want to do but can't; it is what you should not do because it will hurt you—and hurt you bad. . . . God is not a policeman; he is a Father concerned about his children. When a child picks up a snake and the father says, "Put that down right this minute!" the child thinks he's losing a toy. The fact is, he is not losing a toy; he is losing a snake.

—Steve Brown
(Discipline, Correction)

People in general, Christian people in particular, tend to divide sins into two categories: their sins and our sins. The Bible, of course, knows no such distinction. Sin is sin, without partiality shown to the sins of God's people—our sins.

—Joe Bayly
(Judgment, Guilt)

Whenever God touches sin it is independence that is touched, and that awakens resentment in the human heart. Independence must be blasted clean out, there must be no such thing left, only freedom, which is very different. Freedom is the ability not to insist on my rights, but to see that God gets his.

—Oswald Chambers
(Independence, Freedom)

Solitude

We seem so frightened today of being alone that we never let it happen. Instead of planting our solitude with our own dream blossoms, we choke the space with continuous music, chatter, and companionship to which we do not even listen. When the noise stops there is no inner music to take its place. —Anne Morrow Lindbergh
(Quiet, Fear)

Sorrow

There is no despair so absolute as that which comes with the first moments of our first great sorrow, when we have not yet known what it is to have suffered and be healed, to have despaired and recovered hope. —George Eliot
(Grief, Suffering)

Soul

The meaning of earthly existence lies, not as we have grown used to thinking, in prospering, but in the development of the soul.
—Alexander Solzhenitsyn
(Prosperity, Character)

The soul is the place where man's supreme and final battles are fought.
—Abraham Neuman
(Character, Sin)

In a certain sense, every single human soul has more meaning and value than the whole history with its empires, its wars and revolutions, its blossoming and fading civilizations.
—Nicholas Berdyaev
(Evangelism, Human Nature)

What lies behind us and what lies before us are tiny matters compared to what lies within us.
—Ralph Waldo Emerson
(Past, Future)

Speech

When the heart is afire, some sparks will fly out of the mouth.
—Thomas Fuller
(Passion, Unction)

I have learned this art: When I have nothing more to say, I stop talking.
—Martin Luther
(Preaching, Self-control)

Spiritual Disciplines

Most of the significant things done in the world were done by persons who were either too busy or too sick! There are few ideal and leisurely settings for the disciplines of growth. —Robert Thornton Henderson
(Growth, Difficulty)

Spiritual Gifts

Some people have the notion that following your spiritual gifts is spending the days and years of your life doing only those things which come naturally, easily, with no effort, discipline, or practice. —Wesley Tracy
(Discipline, Growth)

Spirituality

Spirituality is a slippery term, but the phenomenon itself is not new. Christian spirituality is nothing other than life in Christ by the presence and power of the Spirit: being conformed to the person of Christ, and being united in communion with God and with others. Spirituality is not an aspect of Christian life, it is the Christian life. —Michael Downey
(Christianity, Holiness)

Success

Those who know how to win are much more numerous than those who know how to make proper use of their victories. —Polybius
(Victory, Responsibility)

159

While no man has succeeded . . . without some spark of divine fire, many have succeeded better by taking precious good care of a precious small spark than others, who have been careless with a generous flame.

—Henry Holt
(Responsibility, Carelessness)

There is nothing so weak, for working purposes, as this enormous importance attached to immediate victory. There is nothing that fails like success.   —G. K. Chesterton
(Victory, Failure)

Nothing fails quite so totally as success without God.

—Vic Pentz
(Failure, God)

I don't think God is too interested in our success. He is interested in our maturity.   —Fred Smith
(Growth, Maturity)

Suffering

He who can't endure the bad will not live to see the good.   —Yiddish proverb
(Trials, Misfortune)

People get very upset by the idea that their children might have to suffer. Well, why . . . are you having children? You want them to be Christians, don't you? If they are going to be Christians, they are going to suffer. That is what life is about.   —Stanley Hauerwas
(Children, Parenting)

We do not want suffering; we want success. We identify not with those who are low and hurt but with those who are high and healthy. We don't like lepers or losers very well; we prefer climbers and comers. For Christians, the temptation to be conformed to this world is desperately sweet and strong. Yet, says the apostle Paul, we are children of God if we suffer with Christ.

—Cornelius Plantinga, Jr.
(Success, Conformity)

Preach to the suffering, and you will never lack a congregation. There is a broken heart in every pew.

—Joseph Parker
(Ministry, Compassion)

Perhaps the main task of the minister is to prevent people from suffering for the wrong reasons.

—Henri Nouwen
(Ministry, Prevention)

It is a fact of Christian experience that life is a series of troughs and peaks. In his efforts to get permanent possession of a soul, God relies on the troughs more than the peaks. And some of his special favorites have gone through longer and deeper troughs than anyone else.

—Peter Marshall, Sr.
(Difficulty, Trials)

161

Supernatural

Surely we cannot take an open question like the super-natural and shut it with a bang, turning the key of the mad-house on all the mystics of history. You cannot take the region called the unknown and calmly say that though you know nothing about it, you know that all the gates are locked.
—G. K. Chesterton
(Agnosticism, Faith)

Surrender

One does not surrender a life in an instant. That which is lifelong can only be surrendered in a lifetime.
—Jim Elliot
(Life, Endurance)

I became my own only when I gave myself to Another.
—C. S. Lewis
(Devotion, Allegiance)

Teaching

Becoming an effective teacher is simple. You just prepare
and prepare until drops of blood appear on your fore-
head. —Marlene LeFever
(Preparation, Devotion)

Teamwork

"What makes a good manager?" someone asked Yogi
Berra. "A good ball club," Yogi replied.
(Leadership, Church)

None of us is as smart as all of us.
—Unknown
(Community, Church)

If the team wins, we all had a good year; if we don't
win, then it doesn't matter who had a good year.
—Paul O'Neill
1994 American League batting champion
(Winning, Success)

Television

The answer [to television] is not censorship, but more citizenship in the corporate boardroom and more active families who will turn off the trash, boycott the sponsors, and tell the executives that you hold them personally responsible for making money from glorifying violence and human degradation.

—Bill Bradley, former U.S. Senator
(Violence, Responsibility)

Temptation

The trouble with trouble is that it usually starts out as a whole lot of fun.

—Anonymous
(Sin, Entertainment)

An untempted minister will never do us any good, and an untried man will talk over our heads.

—Joseph Parker
(Character, Preaching)

Tenderness

The higher people are in the favor of God, the more tender they are.

—Martin Luther
(Compassion, Mercy)

Good Friday came after Christmas, but the angels still sang at the manger. In the midst of the hardest reality of life, there is always a welcome for tenderness and beauty.

—Bruce W. Thielemann
(Easter, Christmas)

Testimony

Preach the gospel at all times. If necessary, use words.

—Francis of Assisi
(Righteousness, Lifestyle)

Time

Don't let yesterday use up too much of today.

—Will Rogers
(Regret, Busyness)

Time is life—nothing more, nothing less. The way you spend your hours and your days is the way you spend your life.

—John Boykin
(Stewardship, Faithfulness)

The management of time is the management of self; therefore, if you manage time with God, he will begin to manage you.

—Jill Briscoe
(Self-control, Devotional Life)

I have this minute in my control. It is all I really do have to work with. It is as magnificent or drab or vile as the thoughts which fill it. I fear our most common sin is empty minutes.

—Frank Laubach
(Stewardship, Sin)

Today

One today is worth two tomorrows.

—Benjamin Franklin
(Present, Future)

Tongue

Ninety percent of the friction of daily life is caused by the wrong tone of voice.

—Francois de la Rochefoucauld
(Speech, Attitude)

The tongue of man is a twisty thing.

—Homer
(Deception, Speech)

Trials

We grow and mature spiritually through adversity—not when everything is going smoothly. . . . [I]n a time of adversity or trouble, the Christian has the opportunity to know God in a special and personal way.

—C. Everett Koop
Former U.S. Surgeon General
(Adversity, Growth)

These are just speed bumps on the highway of life.

—Andrew Wainrib
Los Angeles restaurant owner who lost a
nightclub in the Rodney King verdict riots,
a Malibu home in the fires, and a
beachside cafe in the earthquake.
(Adversity, Attitude)

I have nothing to offer but blood, toil, tears, and sweat.

—Winston Churchill
(Sacrifice, Work)

Trouble

Trouble shared is trouble halved.

—Dorothy Sayers
(Friendship, Grief)

Sentimentalism is born among the flowers; noble senti-
ment is born among the snows.　　—John Henry Jowett
(Wisdom, Sentimentalism)

Truth
He who begins by loving Christianity better than truth
will proceed by loving his own sect or church better
than Christianity, and end in loving himself better than
all.　　—Samuel Taylor Coleridge
(Devotion, Christianity)

The truth does not change according to our ability to
stomach it.　　—Flannery O'Connor
(Courage, Relativity)

The very amount of information that computers make
available threatens us with cognitive overload: overwhelmed with facts, people tend to mistake data for
truth, knowledge for wisdom. With a mind-set fixed on
information, our attention span shortens. We collect
fragments. We become mentally poorer in overall meaning.　　—Michiko Katkutani
(Significance, Information)

Hard are the ways of truth, and rough to walk.
　　—John Milton
(Courage, Honesty)

I never give 'em hell. I just tell the truth, and they think
it's hell.　　—Harry S. Truman
(Speech, Honesty)

Truth does not blush.

—Tertullian
(Conviction, Honesty)

Western culture has made a fundamental change in its religious base. We have exchanged that one who said, "I am the Truth" (John 14:6) for the incredibly expensive doctrine of Freud and the words of all his various disciples. Our new religion says with Pontius Pilate, "What is truth?" and teaches that our status is one of "original victim" rather than "original sin."

—Carol Tharp
(Religion, Blame)

A man can't be always defending the truth; there must be a time to feed on it.

—C. S. Lewis
(Spiritual Growth, Apologetics)

You shall know the truth, and the truth shall make you mad.

—Aldous Huxley
(Honesty, Anger)

Peace, if possible, but the truth at any rate.

—Martin Luther
(Peace, Honesty)

Unbelievers

God is not hostile to sinners, but only to unbelievers.

—Martin Luther
(Sin, Grace)

Understanding

Understanding someone properly involves learning from him, and learning from someone properly involves changing oneself.

—Hans Küng
(Change, Learning)

God, help us not to despise or oppose what we do not understand.

—William Penn
(Unity, Acceptance)

Unity

Talk about *what* you believe and you have disunity.
Talk about *who* you believe in and you have unity.
—E. Stanley Jones
(Belief, Conflict)

Unselfishness

What does the Lord do to help broaden my horizons and assist me in seeing how selfish I am? Very simple: He gives me four busy kids who step on shoes, wrinkle clothes, spill milk, lick car windows, and drop sticky candy on the carpet. . . . Being unselfish in attitude strikes at the very core of our being. It means we are willing to forgo our own comfort, our own preferences, our own schedule, our own desires for another's benefit. And that brings us back to Christ.
—Charles Swindoll
(Parenting, Grace)

170

Values

Even those who have renounced Christ's way and attack
it, in their innermost being still follow Christ's ideals, for
hitherto neither their subtlety nor the ardor of their
hearts has been able to create a higher idea of man and
of virtue than the ideal given by Christ of old. When it
has been attempted, the result has been only grotesque.
—Fyodor Dostoyevsky
(Christianity, Ideals)

People do not value sunsets because they cannot pay for
them.
—Oscar Wilde
(Materialism, Money)

Virtue

He who is not angry at sin is not in love with virtue.
—James Strachan
(Anger, Sin)

I must be poor and in want, before I can exercise the virtue of gratitude; miserable and in torment, before I can exercise the virtue of patience.　　　—John Donne
(Gratitude, Patience)

How commonly vices pass themselves off as virtues. Inordinate laxity is believed to be loving-kindness, and unbridled wrath is accounted the virtue of spiritual zeal. Hence it is necessary for the ruler of souls to distinguish with vigilant care between virtues and vices.
—Gregory the Great
(Anger, Laziness)

Vision

People grow old only by deserting their ideals. Years may wrinkle the skin, but to give up interest wrinkles the soul. Worry, self-doubt, self-distrust, fear and despair; these are the long, long years that bow the head and turn the growing spirit back to dust.
—Douglas MacArthur
(Age, Attitude)

We are like dwarfs, seated on the shoulders of giants. We see more things than the Ancients, things more distant, but it is due neither to the sharpness of our sight nor the greatness of our stature. It is simply because they have lent us their own.　　　—Bernard of Chartres
(Church, Saints)

Leaders do not have to be the greatest visionaries themselves. The vision may come from anyone. The leaders
do have to state the vision, however. Leaders also have
to keep the vision before the people and remind them of
the progress that is being made to achieve the vision.
Otherwise, the people might assume that they are failing
and give up. —Ezra Earl Jones
(Leadership, Communication)

The real danger in our situation lies in the fact that so
many people see clearly what they are revolting from
and so few see at all what they are revolting to.
—Harry Emerson Fosdick
(Revolt, Conformity)

Waiting

Don't wait for your ship to come in; swim out to it.
—Unknown
(Risk, Achievement)

Wealth

Wealth takes away the sharp edges of our moral sensitivities and allows a comfortable confusion about sin and virtue.
—Henri Nouwen
(Materialism, Deception)

I continually find it necessary to guard against that natural love of wealth and grandeur which prompts us always, when we come to apply our general doctrine to our own case, to claim an exception.
—William Wilberforce
(Possessions, Materialism)

Will

The receiving of the Word consists of two parts: attention of mind and intention of will. —William Ames
(Word of God, Obedience)

Winning

About the only problem with success is that it doesn't teach you how to deal with failure. —Tommy Lasorda
(Failure, Success)

Often the best way to win is to forget to keep score.
—Marianne Espinosa
(Competition, Cooperation)

Wisdom

Whatever withdraws us from the power of our senses; whatever makes the past, the distant, the future, predominate over the present, advances us in the dignity of thinking beings. —Samuel Johnson
(Past, Future)

I do not feel obliged to believe that the same God who has endowed us with sense, reason, and intellect has intended us to forgo their use. —Galileo
(Reason, Apologetics)

God's wisdom is not first counsel on how to practice family values or to use common sense. It is the wisdom of his plan of grace, the wisdom of the Cross. That wisdom is foolishness to the calculations of prudence.
—Edmund P. Clowney
(Grace, Sacrifice)

A man has made at least a start on discovering the meaning of human life when he plants shade trees under which he knows full well he will never sit.   —D. Elton Trueblood
(Patience, Service)

Witness

Lord, shine in me and so be in me that all with whom I come in contact may know thy presence in my soul. Let them look up and see no longer me but only Jesus.
—John Henry Newman
(God's Presence, Jesus)

Some of us who have already begun to break the silence of the night have found that the calling to speak is often a vocation of agony, but we must speak. We must speak with all the humility that is appropriate to our limited vision, but we must speak.   —Martin Luther King, Jr.
(Preaching, Social Action)

Women

Men are like the earth and we are like the moon; we turn always one side to them and they think there is no other.   —Olive Schreiner
(Marriage, Men)

Woman—last at the cross, and earliest at the grave.
—E. S. Barrett
(Easter, Devotion)

Whatever women do they must do twice as well as men to be thought half as good. Luckily, this is not difficult.
—Charlotte Whitton
(Work, Marriage)

A woman with a woman's viewpoint is of more value than when she forgets she's a woman and begins to act like a man.
—Nelly Ptaschkina
(Identity, Culture)

Wonder

The world is not lacking in wonders, but in a sense of wonder.
—G. K. Chesterton
(Miracles, Creation)

Faith is the inborn capacity to see God behind everything, the wonder that keeps you an eternal child. Wonder is the very essence of life. Beware always of losing the wonder, and the first thing that stops wonder is religious conviction. Whenever you give a trite testimony, the wonder is gone. The evidence of salvation is that the sense of wonder is developing.
—Oswald Chambers
(Testimony, Faith)

Words

If a man's life be lightning, his words are thunder.
—Medieval proverb
(Spiritual Power, Character)

A man of words and not of deeds
Is like a garden full of weeds.

—Anonymous
(Good Works, Hypocrisy)

Word of God

When the hot Word of God is poured over a cold, cold world, things break, and it is into that brokenness that we are called, into whatever big or small piece we find in front of us, with fire in our bones, to show a frightened world that it is not the heat of the fire that we fear, but the chill that lies ahead if the fire goes out.

—Barbara Brown Taylor
(Courage, Conviction)

When the soul is suffering . . . there is great need of the Word.

—John Chrysostom
(Suffering, Discipleship)

Work

There is a danger of doing too much as well as of doing too little. Life is not for work, but work for life, and when it is carried to the extent of undermining life or unduly absorbing it, work is not praiseworthy but blameworthy.

—Ralph Turnbull
(Balance, Life)

The best kept secret in America today is that people would rather work hard for something they believe in than enjoy a life of pampered idleness.

—John W. Gardner
(Idleness, Purpose)

Do not confound work and fruit. There may be a good deal of work for Christ that is not the fruit of the heavenly Vine.

—Andrew Murray
(Fruitfulness, Busyness)

179

Choose that employment or calling in which you may be most serviceable to God. Choose not that in which you may be most rich or honorable in the world; but that in which you may do most good, and best escape sinning.
—Richard Baxter
(Lifestyle, Vocation)

The highest reward for man's toil is not what he gets for it, but what he becomes by it.
—John Ruskin
(Character, Reward)

Thanks be to God for a life full-packed with things that matter crying to be done—a life, thank God, of never-ending strife against the odds. . . . Just enough time to do one's best, and then pass on, leaving the rest to him.
—John Oxenham
(Stress, Significance)

It is possible to be so active in the service of Christ as to forget to love him. Many a man preaches Christ but gets in front of him by the multiplicity of his own works. . . . Christ can do without your works; what he wants is you. Yet if he really has you, he will have all your works.
—P. T. Forsyth
(Good Works, Devotion)

O Lord, renew our spirits and draw our hearts unto thyself, that our work may not be to us a burden, but a delight; and give us such a mighty love to thee as may sweeten all our obedience.
—Benjamin Jenks
(Love, Obedience)

Most middle-class Americans tend to worship their
work, to work at their play, and to play at their worship.
—Gordon Dahl
(Priorities, Worship)

Disciplined reflection does not take time away from
work; it sustains the spirit and increases the intensity
and quality of work.
—Kesharan Nair
(Discipline, Reflection)

Work as if you were to live 100 years; pray as if you
were to die tomorrow.
—Benjamin Franklin
(Prayer, Future)

I long to accomplish a great and noble task; but it is my
chief duty and joy to accomplish humble tasks as
though they were great and noble. The world is moved
along, not only by the mighty shoves of its heroes, but
also by the aggregate of the tiny pushes of each honest
worker.
—Helen Keller
(Community, Humility)

If a man is to be called to be a streetsweeper, he should
sweep streets even as Michelangelo painted, or
Beethoven composed music, or Shakespeare wrote poetry. He should sweep streets so well that all the hosts of
heaven and earth will pause to say, "Here lived a great
streetsweeper who did his job well."
—Martin Luther King, Jr.
(Vocation, Devotion)

World

The world is poor because her fortune is buried in the sky and all her treasure maps are of the earth.
—Calvin Miller
(Heaven, Eternity)

He who marries the spirit of the age soon becomes a widower.
—Dean Inge
(Culture, Devotion)

We have a society which is psychiatrized in the same sense in which medieval European society was Christianized, religionized—everything was a matter of religion. Now everything is a matter of psychiatry, from homosexuality, to heroin, to murder.
—Thomas Szasz
(Psychology, Blame)

Worry

The eagle that soars in the upper air does not worry itself how it is to cross rivers.
—Gladys Aylward
(Trust, Spiritual Power)

Three things sap a man's strength: worry, travel, and sin.
—Jewish proverb
(Travel, Sin)

When you have accomplished your daily task, go to sleep in peace; God is awake.
—Victor Hugo
(Rest, Faith)

182

Worship

If worship is just one thing we do, everything becomes mundane. If worship is the one thing we do, everything takes on eternal significance. —Timothy J. Christenson
(Priorities, Significance)

Our greatest claim to nobility is our created capacity to know God, to be in personal relationship with him, to love him and to worship him. Indeed, we are most truly human when we are on our knees before our Creator. —John Stott
(God, Creation)

Worship does not satisfy our hunger for God; it whets our appetite. —Eugene H. Peterson
(Longing, Devotion)

I sit for six days a week like a weaver behind his loom, busily fingering the threads of an intricate pattern. On the seventh day, the church in its worship calls me around in front of the loom to look at the pattern on which I have been working. It bids me compare the design of my days with the pattern shown me on Mount Sinai and the Mount of Olives. Some threads thereupon I have to cut, others I pull more tightly, and most of all, I renew my picture of the whole plan. —Ralph W. Sockman
(Perspective, Holiness)

Worship is a stairway on which there is movement in two directions: God comes to man, and man goes to God. —Daniel Baumann
(God, Human Nature)

Worship renewal does not consist of moving chairs in a circle, rearranging the order of worship, or finding new gimmicks. The heart of worship renewal is a recovery of the power of the Holy Spirit, who enables the congregation to offer praise and thanksgiving to God.

—Robert Webber
(Holy Spirit, Renewal)

Somehow, about forty percent of churchgoers seem to have picked up the idea that "singing in church is for singers." The truth is that "singing is for believers." The relevant question is not "Do you have a voice?" but "Do you have a song?"

—Donald Hustad
(Music, Reverence)

There are entire congregations who worship praise and praise worship but who have not yet learned to praise and worship God in Jesus Christ. The song, the dance, the banners have been accepted as worship instead of being seen as a means of expressing worship.

—Judson Cornwall
(Music, Renewal)

Idolatry is worshiping anything that ought to be used, or using anything that is meant to be worshiped.

—Augustine
(Idolatry, Respect)

Youth

We are only young once. That is all society can stand.
—Bob Bowen
(Maturity, Growth)

I was born in the wrong generation. When I was a young man, no one had any respect for youth. Now I am an old man and no one has any respect for age.
—Bertrand Russell
(Age, Respect)

You are only young once, but you can be immature your whole life.
—A bumper sticker
(Immaturity, Wisdom)

Today's accent may be on youth, but the stress is still on the parents.
—Earl Wilson
(Age, Wisdom)

Youth

As I approve of the youth that has something of the old man in him, so am I no less pleased with an old man that has something of the youth. —Cicero
(Age, Wisdom)

Zeal

Fanaticism consists of redoubling your efforts when you have forgotten your aim.

—George Santayana
(Fanaticism, Enthusiasm)

Index

Bold face indicates major headings
and the pages on which they're found.